reconnected
parenting

reconnected parenting

Healing the Whole Family Nervous System Through Regulation, Breathwork and Play Therapy

EMMA JOHNSTON and ELEANOR MANN

HAY HOUSE

Carlsbad, California • New York City
London • Sydney • New Delhi

Published in the United Kingdom by:
Hay House UK Ltd, 1st Floor, Crawford Corner,
91–93 Baker Street, London W1U 6QQ
Tel: +44 (0)20 3927 7290; www.hayhouse.co.uk

Text © 2025 by Emma Johnston and Eleanor Mann

Cover design: Julie Davison • Interior design: Nick C. Welch
Interior photos illustrations: Dani Hunt / Neverland Studio

The moral rights of the authors have been asserted.

All rights reserved. No part of this book may be reproduced by any mechanical, photographic or electronic process, or in the form of a phonographic recording; nor may it be stored in a retrieval system, transmitted or otherwise be copied for public or private use, other than for 'fair use' as brief quotations embodied in articles and reviews, without prior written permission of the publisher.

The information given in this book should not be treated as a substitute for professional medical advice; always consult a medical practitioner. Any use of information in this book is at the reader's discretion and risk. Neither the authors nor the publisher can be held responsible for any loss, claim or damage arising out of the use, or misuse, of the suggestions made, the failure to take medical advice or for any material on third-party websites.

A catalogue record for this book is available from the British Library

Tradepaper ISBN: 978-1-837-82480-9
E-book ISBN: 978-1-4019-9698-7
Audiobook ISBN: 978-1-4019-9685-7

10 9 8 7 6 5 4 3 2 1

This product uses responsibly sourced papers, including recycled materials and materials from other controlled sources. For more information, see www.hayhouse.co.uk

The authorized representative in the EU for product safety and compliance is Penguin Random House Ireland, Morrison Chambers, 32 Nassau Street, Dublin D02 YH68, Ireland. https://eu-contact.penguin.ie

Printed and bound by CPI Group (UK) Ltd, Croydon CR0 4YY

contents

Chapter 1:	Introduction	1
Chapter 2:	Regulating the Whole Family Nervous System	17
Chapter 3:	First, Let's Take a Slower, Fuller Breath—Eleanor	25

SECTION I: Understanding Your Nervous System

Chapter 4:	Your Nervous System—Eleanor	33
Chapter 5:	The Nervous System Holds the Imprint!—Eleanor	51
Chapter 6:	Parenting, Why Is It So Challenging?—Emma	65
Chapter 7:	The Five Stress Archetypes—Emma	75
Chapter 8:	Embracing the Gifts of Parenting—Emma	93
Chapter 9:	Breath and the Nervous System—Eleanor	101

SECTION II: Understanding Your Child's Nervous System

Chapter 10:	Your Child's Nervous System—Eleanor	125
Chapter 11:	How Do I Help My Kids to Regulate?—Eleanor	141
Chapter 12:	When Can My Kids Self-Regulate?	157
Chapter 13:	The Five Kids Stress Archetypes—Eleanor	171
Chapter 14:	Play Is Regulating—Eleanor	183
Chapter 15:	Regulating Through Play—Eleanor	197

SECTION III: Understanding the Whole Family Nervous System

Chapter 16: Paradigm Shift #1, Attunement: The Invisible Communication Between Parent and Child   213

Chapter 17: Paradigm Shift #2, Interconnection: Children Will Express What the Adults Suppress   231

Chapter 18: Paradigm Shift #3, Eldership: Regulating the Whole Family Nervous System   239

Chapter 19: Conclusion   249

References   251

Endnotes   255

Acknowledgments   261

About the Authors   263

For my children Atlas, Solaris, Venus, Faedra, and Halo. Your presence has expanded me beyond what I ever thought possible. I love you.
— Emma

For Nissa, Uri, Darshan, and Mirabai—my most profound teachers—this book is not just for you, but thanks to the gifts you have all given me.
— Eleanor

CHAPTER 1

Introduction

Many parents, when asked what they think they need for parenting to be easier, will reply, *"To be able to stay calm"* or *"To have a more regulated nervous system"* or *"If my kids could just be more regulated...."*

The nervous system vernacular has slowly but steadily made its way into our everyday language thanks to the considerable amount of research into the nervous system over the past 10 years. Once therapists, yoga teachers, and other wellness professionals started talking about it, the nervous system became a favorite topic among mainstream media pundits and "calm parenting" accounts on social media.

Despite this, you might still be unclear as to why understanding your and your children's nervous systems is important. How is understanding the nervous system helpful for parents?

A better question is actually this . . .

Who here, reading this, struggles to be the parent they want to be when their kids have big feelings, get angry, yell, talk back, whinge, whine, hit, kick, or have big meltdowns that go on for ages?

No doubt every parent or carer reading this has their hand up right now.

These stressful moments are the times when it's really easy to also lose our cool and for all the gentle parenting to go right out the window. It is in these moments we can find ourselves resorting to threats or punishments, bribes or rewards.

Or you might find yourself even just questioning whether gentle parenting works; after all, you had kept your cool for hours, and no one listened to you, and now that you are yelling as well, they seem to be listening a bit more!

And so, here's the thing. . . .

Generally, we struggle with our children's behavior when we're overwhelmed or angry about the way they are behaving, or we are finding parenting all too much. On some level, in those moments we are subconsciously relating to our kids as though they are intentionally choosing to behave the way that they are behaving and that we are failing in some way!

Maybe you have even thought to yourself, *"They're manipulating me!"* or *"If they could just listen to me and do as I say, then they wouldn't be so upset"* or *"If I was stricter, they would know they should listen to me!"*

This can seem especially true if our kids seem to stop whining or acting out when we *do* lose our cool and yell at them or have our own tantrum! The thing is, when we understand what our kids' behavior is expressing from the lens of their neurobiology—that is, from what is happening in their nervous system—then we really understand that they are always doing the best they can with what they've got available to them.

This new perspective is a paradigm shift for us on a day-to-day level. Why?

Well, let's just think about that for a second. How would *your* day-to-day life change if you could authentically respond to your kids with a deep understanding that "my child is doing the best they can with what they've got"?

Let's try and imagine the difference for a moment.

Let's say your child has been whining and whinging, and normally, you would start to feel pretty frustrated or worn down after a while. What would be different about the way you responded to them if you really understood that they are doing the best they can with what they've got?

Introduction

Well, over the last five years, we've asked tens of thousands of parents this question, so we can tell you what the most common answers are:

"I could be more patient."

"I could be more present."

"I would be more playful."

"I would have the energy to be with them and to help them rather than to punish or control or do anything to just make the behavior go away."

And one of our favorites: *"We would laugh more often as a family."*

And isn't that just what we want as parents? To be able to be free to choose our responses in the moments when we would normally react or overreact, yell, feel helpless, or be overwhelmed by our kids' behaviors?

What difference would it make to your household if you could laugh more often, be more playful with your kids, and just enjoy your time as a family together? Would that change the game at your house?

Our kids are not the only ones doing the best they can with what they've got! There is someone else who is also working to the capacity of their nervous system, and that is you! Let's unpack this a bit.

Many parents we speak to are very self-aware parents (if you are reading this, it is likely you are too!).

Maybe you can notice when you are starting to get upset, or perhaps you have done enough therapy to know why you react when your kids do certain things, or you might do a lot of meditation, mindfulness, or yoga, or maybe you already follow a lot of gentle parenting accounts on Instagram or TikTok, or have read all the books, listened to podcasts, and have a list of scripts and know exactly what you should do and say in those moments when your kids are acting out.

We are willing to bet that more often than not, in the moments that really matter, those hard moments when you feel like parenting is bringing you to your knees because you're sleep-deprived or the crying has been going for ages or because they are pushing a button that always sets you off, I am guessing that it is in those moments you struggle to choose the way you want to respond.

When you have reached your limit, no parenting script and not even self-awareness can make a difference.

Often this means that when we want to be a conscious, gentle parent, we can find that parenting feels even more stressful because, while we might *know* better, we simultaneously cannot actually *do* better when it matters.

When self-awareness is coupled with the inability to choose the way you want to respond during stressful moments, it can load up parents with a huge feeling of incompetence and failure!

Over the years, we have met many parents who are despairing and desperate to see some concrete change in their reactions, especially if they have read all the books or have been doing self-awareness work for some time.

We've found the very first step to being authentically free to choose your response in the moment (hint: that's the end goal for what this book is going to give you!) is to understand (and heal) your nervous system.

Humor us for a moment, and pause to reflect on what would change for you just with the new understanding, *"I am doing the best I can with what I have available to me right now."*

We are guessing you would feel a lot less pressure, maybe feel more centered, more self-accepting, and have more inner space where you are free to choose your response.

Over the course of this book, we are excited to show you what we have found to be the missing piece behind why we can know better but not *do* better in the moments that count

Introduction

with our kids, and we are going to take you on an embodied understanding of your nervous system. We'll show you why your breath can rewire your reactions from your body up, creating deep, lasting change.

This transformation happens from the inside out, on a neurobiological level, resulting in a whole new Autonomic Baseline and outlook on stressful life situations. Then you can show up as a parent in a way that aligns with your highest visions. You move beyond learning scripts and what you think you "should" do and instead respond from a place of freedom, authenticity, and spaciousness.

For your kids, we are diving into the world of play, helping you to understand what is happening behind your child's behavior and showing you how your child's play also reflects what is happening in their nervous system.

A real eye-opener for people is realizing that play for our children has a similar healing effect to when we, as adults, practice breathwork. As you'll see later on, these two practices, play and breathwork, provide a safe space to release stored stress while also guiding us back to our true nature.

The Reconnected Parenting model of the Whole Family Nervous System is a unique perspective that takes parents from feeling disconnected to reconnecting with their authentic self so they can be free to respond the way they really want to and create a life of ease and enjoyment in their family life.

We are going to show you how although the nervous system matures with age, we can still get stuck in arrested states of development, and why maturing into adult and elder nervous-system states determines your sense of connection to others and to your intuition. We'll also explain why our main goal should be to be safe to feel all our feelings, not just to be calm all the time.

Before we dive into this, first we'd love to share our experiences of parenting and how we came to be sharing this with you here.

Meet Eleanor

Hi, I am Eleanor, and I am a counselor, play therapist, and breathwork teacher trainer. However, to give you a better sense of how I came to be here, my story really starts when I became a parent back in 2002! I am the mother of four kids, ages 16 to 22 at the time of writing this book, and a stepdaughter who is 24 *(yes, I officially have adult children, which still blows my mind!).*

When my eldest children were born back in 2002 and 2004, I didn't have any of the tools I have today. There was no social media at the time. In order to find enlightened parenting information, you kind of had to bump into someone or get lucky with finding a book!

To be honest, though, I didn't really know that I was missing anything because, for the first year or so, I found parenting to be pretty effortless.

I could be patient. I could be kind. I was playful and fun. I felt on top of all the important things; we ate organic food, wore natural fibers, had only wooden toys and handmade things, and watched no TV. I'm sure you can imagine the whole vibe. I felt like I had this parenting thing in the bag!

And then something changed after my second son was born.

When he was almost one and old enough to learn to stand, his little legs wobbled as he practiced pulling up on all the things—absolutely at that adorable age. My eldest daughter (who was two and a half at the time) went through a phase where she would come literally running to push him over every time he got close to succeeding.

Introduction

And it was the first time I felt real anger toward one of my children, and—*it shocked me.*

You know that feeling when you have a little baby, and you think to yourself, *"I'm always going to be kind and loving toward you. I am going to take such good care of you,"* and you make all of these promises to yourself about the way you will parent. Then, inevitably, we find ourselves in a moment where difficult emotions are triggered, and it can be really challenging and shocking.

The first time I felt angry at my kids, I was really confronted by just how rageful I felt! It felt totally out of my own control, and even when I would plan for how I would respond better next time, I would still find myself feeling angry and regretting it!

Around this time, quite by accident, I discovered breathwork.

I had gone to a drumming class that spontaneously turned into a breathwork session at the end. The guide asked for volunteers to demonstrate the process, and something made me put up my hand. Well, little did I know how much that moment would change the course of my life!

During the breathwork, I had a profound experience of getting in touch with what was really driving the anger I was feeling when my daughter was pushing over my son. A veil lifted, and I saw with complete clarity what was happening for me unconsciously at that moment. Underneath my anger at my daughter was my own suppressed anger from when my younger sibling was born, bubbling underneath like a volcano. She was five years younger than me, and while I didn't have any specific negative memory, what was with me every moment of the day was the body memory of anger and confusion that I felt when our family changed when she arrived!

Every time my daughter pushed over her sibling, my own unintegrated feelings bubbled up and over.

I was no longer a child, but the big "inner child" feelings remained, still as overwhelming as they were when I was little, and I was completely reactive and in their grip once they had been triggered. This moment of awareness and insight was a pivotal moment for me.

After I had had the realization, I looked bewildered around me to the facilitator and said, *"But I've already had kids,"* and the second thing was, *"No one told me."* See, I had realized something more than just the presence of my own suppressed anger.

I also saw with absolute clarity that because I was suppressing my own anger, I had to suppress my daughter's, and so the suppression of anger was being passed down to her. Anger wasn't okay for me to feel, and so I unconsciously had to try and stop my daughter from expressing the same thing! To avoid my own feelings!

I was absolutely shocked that not one single person had told me that I would not be able to be with my kids in emotions where no one had been there for me when I was little. I was mind-blown. I knew I would never see myself, my kids, or the world in the same way again.

This experience alone sparked my fascination with conscious living, with healing, and with breathwork, but it was what unfolded afterward when I got home that really cemented it for me. When I went back into my life after that session, the next time she ran to push him over, I saw what was really going on *underneath the behavior,* and I felt so much compassion for her. I could understand the message about what she needed underneath. I could relate to her in the present moment, and I could respond to her in the way that I wanted and that she needed. The moment was transformed.

After this, I went on to train in breathwork, and I was absolutely hooked on making my unconscious relationship to the world conscious from that point on. To date, I have been practicing breathwork myself for over 20 years now, and

Introduction

professionally, I have supported tens of thousands of people. What was amazing, though, was just like the way that breathwork showed up in my own life at the exact right time, it seems that I had shown up at the exact right time in the history of breathwork's timeline also!

At the time, breathwork was not widely known. It was a very alternative practice that was not something many people had heard of. To be honest, most people thought the idea of breathwork was a bit weird. This is hard to imagine with the recent popularity of conscious breathing practices! At the time of writing, it seems like everyone is doing it.

A recent SEO search suggested that in the past 10 years, Google searches for breathwork have increased by 700 percent! And that search will find you a myriad of practices. Today there is breathwork for everything from peak sport performance to spiritual awakening, and despite the differences, almost all will reference the benefit that conscious breathing has on the nervous system.

When my kids became old enough for school, I had the time to complete a counseling degree and start working as a family counselor. After about 10 years, as they grew and I had more time for things, I found a drive to keep learning, so I went back to school to study psychology. As I came toward the end of the psych degree, the time came to consider a topic for my own contribution to the field of psychology research. Thanks to the boom of research into mindfulness and meditation, and the development of theories like polyvagal theory, it was a natural next step to spend my time specializing in the nervous system and the breath. This time was thrilling, in part because the literature was validating my personal and spiritual journey, but also because conscious breathing was at the beginning of becoming mainstream.

Now, around this time, the other thing that had caught my fascination was play therapy. I was working alongside a very inspiring play therapist, and the stories she told about her children in play therapy sounded like those I had personally experienced only in breathwork—and certainly never through talk therapy with my clients. So I trained in child-centered play therapy and was just so moved by the power of play and of children's innate wisdom. Daily, I witnessed how integrating hardship came naturally to the kids I was working with—they just needed the space and support to process their experiences through playing! It was obvious that, like my daughter, the adults around them could not tolerate their feelings, and this was most of what was stopping them from healing!

And unlike adults who often took a long time before they were safe enough to feel supressed emotions, I noticed that children were very open and receptive to feeling and changing!

In the initial stages of practicing, my play therapy mentor and supervisor made a fascinating comment that piqued my interest about the synergy between breath and play. When you are training in play therapy, it's common practice to video yourself while you do sessions and get feedback from master therapists. My supervisor asked me in the first few weeks of practicing, *"How long have you been doing this?"* She continued, saying, *"You are tuning in to the children's behavior in a way that I only see in some people after twenty, thirty years of practice, and some people never get there."* I knew instantly what she was noticing was my deeply attuned relationship to my nervous system because of my years of breathwork. The breath practice and my elder nervous system were able to support kids to go deeper into their own nervous-system integration through play.

Looking back now, these days were exciting beginnings in experiencing what we now call the Whole Family Nervous System, but more on that later, because the other thing that happened at about this time was, I met Emma!

Introduction

Meet Emma

My name is Emma, and many have known me over the years as New Earth Mama on Instagram. My journey into conscious parenting began when I was expecting my first son, Atlas.

I was determined to follow my own path in parenting; I wanted to do things totally different from the way I was brought up!

I knew I wanted to raise my kids in a way that kept them in touch with their innocence, playfulness, and spiritual senses. I wanted to co-sleep and stay home with them in the early years. I wanted them to feel safe and held each day of their young lives.

Don't get me wrong. My parents are lovely, honest, caring people. They did the absolute best they could. But my father was a war veteran who'd never done any work on healing his profound trauma, and a lot of the family pressure fell on my mum, which left her depleted, stressed, and truly neurotic sometimes.

While I have so much compassion now, when I was pregnant, I remember saying a few times, "I'm going to do it differently."

The first year of being a mum to Atlas was divine.

I felt like I was nailing it; I'd had the dream home birth. He was a dream to be with every day. He was gorgeous, and I was literally in love with parenting. I'd read all the gentle/conscious parenting books, and on a cognitive level, I knew exactly what being a gentle parent should look like. In those first 18 months, I was the poster parent (in my own mind) of conscious parenting.

Then he became a toddler, and I had this moment where he did something cheeky. I was stressed, and I yelled at him. What shook me the most in this moment was I had this very weird experience of looking at him while getting angry and feeling like I was looking through my mother's eyes!

I was shocked. I thought I was doing things differently.

That moment absolutely shook me. I realized I had work to do!

I started seeing a kinesiologist and thought, *"Maybe this is what I need!"* So I began a double diploma in kinesiology and mind-body medicine, and for the very first time, I learned that our body stores emotions. It really blew my mind because it showed me so much about what was going on for me on a much deeper level around my suppressed emotions.

My path was opening up a bit; I was learning more about the metaphysical realities of life, and I was starting to learn different ways of being.

I really, really loved learning kinesiology, but I had this feeling like there was something else. So, very, very randomly, I landed in breathwork training.

I had no idea what I was signing myself up for.

Somehow, the money came to me in a very synchronous, bizarre way—a gift! That ended up being the exact amount of money I needed to do the training. I trusted the synchronicity, and I landed in breathwork training.

That is where I realized I couldn't even get in touch with tears.

I spent the whole week of this particular stuck in the reality that I couldn't cry! I felt really upset, but I couldn't express it.

I had these flooding memories of my father always shutting down my tears. He would repeat "stop crying" over and over when I was upset. He couldn't handle the tears, and so I shut down that part of myself. No wonder I was getting triggered by my kids' big emotions! I couldn't even be with my own feelings! I was hooked on breathwork from those first experiences and went on to study rebirthing breathwork, including underwater rebirthing, which taps into the stored memory of our time within the womb. This gave me an unbelievable leap onto an entirely new trajectory.

Introduction

It was around the time of welcoming my second son, Solaris, that I connected with Eleanor, who introduced me to Connected Play, the play therapy model we now teach families in Reconnected Parenting. This revolutionary concept of play being the healing balm children naturally use to unwind stress, combined with my deep immersion in breathwork, transformed my approach to parenting.

I had the most magical experience of using Connected Play the very day my second baby was born.

Atlas had fallen asleep the night before, missing Solaris's birth. When he woke up, I could see on his face that he was confused, upset, and alarmed that this squishy little newborn was suddenly going to be sticking around. He ended up having a 45-minute meltdown over the color of the bowl we served his breakfast in, but Connected Play had given me a bigger awareness. It wasn't about the bowl; it was his grief and upset about this new baby arriving. His world was being rocked!

I used that moment to really see, hear, and acknowledge the huge feelings that were happening for him, using the reflective tools I'd learned from Connected Play. And I believe in retrospect, that moment allowed Atlas to accept his new sibling into the family with more ease. After that meltdown, and our connection in the moment, he has gone on to absolutely love his younger brother, and now they are the best of friends with no jealousy or hard feelings. It also made me ponder, *why* don't parents know this magic?

Why is this play therapy wisdom kept only for play therapists when parents could be with their kids in this way themselves? That's why I was a huge *yes* when Eleanor reached out to me about the beginnings of an idea for a program called Reconnected Parenting.

It was our combined love of breathwork and this way of being with kids that has built Reconnected Parenting to be the most incredible community of parents who are truly doing "the work" of unwinding stored stress from their own childhoods and learning new ways to be with their kids that are building a new paradigm of awareness in a massive ripple across the globe.

I've now birthed five beautiful children, and I have found that each of my children has propelled me further toward personal evolution, unlocking deeper layers of myself and guiding me toward a more conscious and authentic way of showing up for them and the world. My dedication to breathwork and the transformational impact it has had on my life has led me to share my experiences and insights with a global audience, inspiring others on their own parenting journeys.

I see how the years of self-discovery that breathwork has uncovered has made me more available to the present moment, has made me a creator of my life, and has ultimately shifted the way my family interacts with one another. It's such a change from what I experienced growing up. Being able to "hold the space" for my family, being the nervous system everyone is borrowing from, allows me to ensure everyone in the family gets seen and acknowledged, leading to deeper connections and, overall, more family flow and ease.

This book is about going deeper than the current parenting paradigm, even deeper than the conscious parenting paradigm!

What is next?

No matter where you are in life, whether you are thinking about having kids, already have kids, are a grandparent, are an educator or carer, or you work with kids in some capacity . . .

Regardless of whether you are exhausted and stressed, curious about ways you can be a more conscious, self-aware guide for your children, or perhaps just interested in conscious breathing and conscious relating, we welcome you to dive in and explore the transformation that is available to your

Introduction

whole family when you understand the nervous system and how the breath connects you deeper to your body and spirit and relationships.

As you read through the book, you will hear from both of us as we share the perspective of The Reconnected (that is, you will be hearing from the both of us!), and other chapters are from Emma's perspective and, of course, Eleanor's. You will see one of our names at the beginning of the chapter to distinguish who is speaking.

Okay, let's dive in!

CHAPTER 2

Regulating the Whole Family Nervous System

A family is a complex, intertwined, interdependent yet individual, neurobiological, relational, and spiritual system that is in constant communication. There is always far more communication happening in the moment than meets the eye, and our communication goes far beyond the spoken word.

In many ways as a parent, it doesn't matter what words you say; your children will pick up on the emotions and thoughts you are really experiencing deep down, maybe even beyond what you are aware of yourself, and this is happening via their highly sensitive and still-developing nervous systems.

Most parents I've spoken to have experienced this deep sense of attunement to their children and have a story of a time when they have seen it in action, like turning around just in time to stop a toddler from falling over or having a child walk in the room and ask you about something you were only just thinking about.

In the Introduction, we shared some stories of moments where we realized that our childhood "stuff" can be triggered by our kids' behavior. Most conscious parenting, or re-parenting, methods focus on this (*very important*) topic. But it is not the full picture! Emotionally, neurobiologically, and relationally, there are other layers that come into play.

At The Reconnected, we have spent many years researching, practicing, and teaching about these different layers, and over time it has become a model to understand what we now call the Whole Family Nervous System. Most people understand the nervous system as being relevant for emotional regulation and stress (and yes, we will cover this as well), but many people do not realize that every individual also has a social nervous system that tracks along with our felt sense of being connected with our family! This means most parents have no awareness that the Whole Family Nervous System is activated when:

- You feel yourself getting tense when your child gets upset about something.
- You're collapsed on the couch at the end of the day, exhausted, and then soon after, the kids start getting absolutely revved up.
- And you know those times when your kids don't listen to what you are saying until you lose it! *Then* they listen. Yep! (When you learn about the nervous system, you will understand the reason this happens as well!)

So, yes, our own childhood "stuff" can drive the reactions we have to our kids from day to day, *but* it might also be an accurate "pick up" of what our kids are experiencing, an unconscious avoidance of our kids' attempts to process an experience that is confronting for us, or to flip it around, your kids may be attempting to bring you back into connection with them. They might be reacting to dysregulation they are picking up in you that you aren't aware of!

Truth is, our nervous systems are in a constant, dynamic conversation with our kids.

Reading all of this, can you get a sense why, when you have tried to stay calm, inside you are actually losing it, or why using

Regulating the Whole Family Nervous System

a calm parenting script through gritted teeth tends to fall flat? Because it's only the surface conversation. The real conversation is happening from nervous system to nervous system.

Mind blown already? We get it—this information changed everything for us—and we haven't even properly started yet!

Now, what if, rather than being unaware of all of this connection, and therefore remaining unconscious to the deeper conversations that are happening nervous system to nervous system, you instead were able to be conscious, aware, and intentional?

What if, instead of trying to fix your kids or yourself at the surface, you could instead begin to tune in to and regulate the Whole Family Nervous System?

There is a more achievable, realistic, and profound truth than trying to mold ourselves into an unrealistic version of the perfect calm parent—and it is that we can use our interconnectedness with our kids and attunement to our nervous system to know intuitively what is really happening in the present moment for ourselves and our kids.

When we do this, we can receive the gifts our children bring us. Often, they are simply calling us to be more connected and present to our true authentic selves—so that they can be too!

This is the true gift of parenting.

A gift that is underneath the daily challenges, when we can view our family as a Whole Family Nervous System.

Over the course of this book, we are going to go on a journey together—step by integrated step! You will come to understand your own nervous system, and your child's, and experience the paradigm shifts in awareness that this understanding brings. You might also be wondering how this can be practically applied to the day-to-day.

Let's hear from some of the Reconnected community members to see how this might help in everyday life!

When we met Jas, she told us that one of her tricky moments was putting her toddler into the car seat. Her daughter never wanted to be put in by her mum: *"She wanted to do it herself."* (If you have a toddler, does this sound familiar?) With a toddler in the strong-willed stage, these moments would leave Jas feeling powerless, helpless, and defeated.

She shared with us recently, *"Knowing that the helplessness and powerlessness I feel when I can't get her to go into her car seat are partly how she is feeling about having no choice about what she is doing, helps me to stop being reactive, as though the feelings are mine. It means I can be really patient with her, to respond with compassion to what I am picking up from her and what it tells me that she needs, and the best part?*

"This kind of understanding and grace takes all the power struggle out of it, and now getting in the car just flows!"

See, when parents know how to distinguish "what is mine" and "what is theirs" and can think to themselves, "What does my child's behavior tell me about what is going on for me, for them, or for the whole family?" then they can communicate in ways that everyone feels safe with.

And powerfully, we can also use this neurobiological information to help our kids go deeper into healing things from the past.

Like Andrea, who was a young mum whose daughter was born at a time when she had very little support.

At bedtime, she said, *"I was very undersupported, and I let her cry. I didn't know that there were other ways of doing things. I just put her in a room, and she'd cry. It's not stuff that I'd ever think about doing now, but at the time I was following what I thought I had to do."*

Over time, with years of self-awareness practice, and with practice in speaking nervous system to nervous system, she was able to recognize when her daughter was triggered from these times of being left alone as a baby.

She said, *"When she was about nine years old, we were still having big meltdowns at bedtime. I noticed she just switches into this rage and wants me to get out of her room, but then she doesn't go to sleep! So, we end up stuck in a loop and often arguing!*

"And the other night, like she was trying to get my attention, and I was doing something else, while she was playing a game with a toy. And she threw it at me to catch it and I wasn't paying attention.

"That was the trigger! And she just flipped.

"And I was like, whoa okay, I can feel what is being said (behind her words!), and I can see there is an opportunity for a healing conversation now."

What happened next is a testament to understanding the Whole Family Nervous System. She was able to help her to heal the emotions that were still there from when she was a baby.

Andrea said to us: *"This moment was significant for me because usually an activated moment like that would have just sent me into not knowing what to say, and in the past I would have just been so hurt and taken things so personally, and most likely punished her!"*

Instead it was healing! For both of them.

Understanding the nervous system—in an embodied way, not just intellectually—means we know that when a child has a meltdown, it is their nervous system talking, not bad behavior. We can see what they are really saying underneath the dysregulation! All through understanding the Whole Family Nervous System. Incredible, huh?

And that is what this book is all about.

Where does this revolutionary perspective come from? Why doesn't everyone know about this already?

As we were writing this book, it became apparent that at The Reconnected we are bringing together a few very different ways of "knowing."

In the West we tend to highly value academic, intellectual understanding and minimize the "knowing" and wisdom that comes directly from within ourselves or our bodies. The real foundation of this work started in 2004, and since then has accumulated in many tens of thousands of hours of personal practice exploring our own nervous systems through the breath. It is also based on thousands of hours spent supporting others to do the same, which has given us a huge amount of experience in the emerging field of conscious breathing.

The second is of course drawing upon scientific theories, research, and evidence from the field of neuroscience, neurobiology, and relational sciences like interpersonal neurobiology.[1] These disciplines give us a deeper understanding of what we know about the nervous system and bring science-informed perspectives on how the NS interacts with relationships and why the breath is so transformative to all areas of our lives. As the play therapist Theresa Kestly suggests, being *science informed* is "honouring and relying on our scientific methods, while simultaneously opening up to those *promising practices* that are emerging out of the rapidly developing field of neuroscience."[2] Breathwork and play therapy are two of those practices.

But there is also a third important "way of knowing" that this book is based on.

At The Reconnected, we value the integrity of your lived experience very highly.

We encourage you to create contemplative moments with the breath to engage in personal reflection and processing as a way of finding your own answers within. As you read we encourage you to be open, trusting what resonates for you, thinking critically (which is different from being closed off and skeptical) and being open to having your own "knowing" or sense of truth activated while you are on an experiential journey with the information, practical tools, and reflection points.

Have you ever read a book, and the whole time you were nodding in resonance like, "*Yes, yes, this is exactly what I have been thinking and experiencing, but I haven't had the words until now*"?

It's like the content feels familiar, even though you are reading it for the first time, and this is because it is ultimately a remembering of what is innately true about human nature and relationships.

These moments often feel synchronistic, or like Carl Jung described, "meaningfully coincidental."

A lot of you have experiences where this type of information comes to you at the exact right time in your life. It is almost like a part of you knew that you needed to hear the words you are reading, at exactly this moment in time, so you can take the next step in your personal journey.

As such, reading this book is a "whole self" experience! One that incorporates what is known currently from science along with your own intuitive sense of knowing what is true for you, rather than only one or the other. One that is informative, as well as experiential, transformational, and soulful.

Section I of this book gives you an understanding of your own nervous system, and Section II will support you to go deeper and connect with your child's nervous system. Section III explores the interconnectedness of families through the Whole Family Nervous System model. At any time, if you would like to watch an instructional video or join a conversation with thousands of other families, you can go to www.thereconnected.com/book.

Thank you for being here with us, at the forefront of a wave of parenting that has the power to change the world!

CHAPTER 3

First, Let's Take a Slower, Fuller Breath—Eleanor

The science is definitely in agreement on this . . . (and I think you will find your body will affirm the same).

The best way to ground down, connect with ourselves, feel calm, think clearer and more positively, be available for our kids, feel in touch with our intuition and "gut knowing" more clearly, be in the present moment, and improve pretty much all areas of our well-being . . .

is to take a slower, fuller-than-usual breath.

Let's do it together now.

On your next inhalation, begin to breathe in and out through your nose.

And then begin to slow your breath right down, and take in more air than you usually would (without straining). Breathe fuller than your usual breath. Let's do it a few times.

Inhale.

Exhale.

Yep, even while you are reading, you can have in the background of your awareness the quality of your breathing, and you can gently, consciously control your breath.

Doesn't that feel good?

If you did manage to follow along, you will likely have felt an instant shift in mood, in how your body feels, and even in the quality of your thoughts.

Whether you are aware of it or not, by doing so, you have activated the relaxation response in your nervous system.

Throughout the book we are going to remind you to breathe and invite you to take pauses to breathe throughout as a way of slowing down to digest and understand the information in this book, as well as staying present and self-aware of your responses to the information you are reading.

So, what is breathwork?

Nowadays, it seems like the whole world is into breathwork or conscious breathing, but what exactly is it?

Maybe you have heard about Wim Hof breathing or tried box breathing or done pranayama at a yoga class. Perhaps you have an idea that breathwork is about relaxation . . . or maybe you have experienced a breathwork class, where people get loudly emotional and try to release their fears and anger all together in big groups.

You are just as likely to hear about breathwork from your doctor or psychologist as you are from someone like a yoga teacher.

The thing is that these days the term *breathwork* is used to describe any type of breathing practice, from yoga breathing (pranayama) to relaxation breathing, from science-based practices to esoteric practices.

And it is not completely accurate!

So, what *is* breathwork?

One of my first breathwork experiences was a holotropic breathwork session back in 2004.

In my first experience with a holotropic-style session, I noticed an incredible change in my understanding about life. I had a 180 shift in my relationship to anger in the moment I was triggered when my daughter was pushing her younger sibling.

And I wanted more!

So I tried all the breathwork I could find.

The first type of breathwork I tried was a fast breath in and out through the mouth, which is (I found out later) designed to give the participant an experience equivalent to taking a mild psychedelic to activate a non-ordinary state of consciousness. In this session I felt like I experienced my soul for the first time, and I felt myself having a profound spiritual experience.

I found out later that this type of breathwork was founded in the '70s by psychiatrist Stanislav Grof, who initially researched the effect of LSD on psychiatric disorders like depression, anxiety, and trauma. When it became illegal to research LSD, he found ways to use the breath and mimic the brain chemistry changes to develop holotropic breathwork—a style that is sweeping the globe in popularity today.

Technically the term *breathwork* was originally used to describe the work of Grof and another pioneer of breathing practices in the West, and then any conscious, connected breathwork style that branched off from one of these two. The second pioneer was a man named Leonard Orr, and he discovered through his own personal explorations that he could use his breath to remember his birth, and he determined through these experiences that birth was an impactful experience that many people still carried stress from as adults. He showed other people how to "rebirth" themselves using a breath style that he called *rebirthing breathwork*. The emphasis was on conscious, connected (circular) breathing and releasing the tension held from birth.

Emma trained in this lineage, and she tells me that in this style the breath is inhaled dynamically in and out through the nose, with no pauses, and you let any sensations build as much as you can with the breath until "catharsis" or Release. Emma said, "It is absolutely incredible how through breathing like this, you can literally get transported straight away to a different age and how healing it is, even though the experience itself can be a lot! If someone had told me that your own birth trauma impacted your entire life, I might have been skeptical. But from my personal experience of using the breath to access birth memory and witnessing others, it blew my mind that fully grown adults were having physical, emotional, and spiritual memories of their birth and learning about things that their parents later confirmed to be true, just from using a connected breath!

I am sure you can appreciate that back in the '80s, '90s, and early 2000s, these practices and perspectives could not have been more fringe, and the general mainstream mindset could not have been more closed off to exploring such strange practices! Even today many of you may be raising your eyebrows in disbelief!

A few years after exploring holotropic breathwork, I discovered a third branch of breathwork that had been developed by Australian breathworker Alakh Analda. She had founded a style of breathwork that took the concepts that the earlier breathwork pioneers had discovered, and through observation of thousands of client sessions and her own experiences of mindful, self-awareness living in a monastery, she slowed the breath down so that the experience was integrative and parasympathetic.

This slower, more relaxed, and subtle way of breathing and the mindful self-awareness aspect of the practice immediately grabbed my attention as a counselor on a professional level.

Here was a practice that had the potential to bridge to the mainstream and that was accessible to everyone.

The term *breathwork* is used to describe any type of controlled breathing practice, but not many people realize that breathwork is technically an umbrella term for practices that come from either holotropic breathwork or rebirthing breathwork.

Another thing that confuses people is, since around 2015, there must have been hundreds of "new" styles of breathwork that had their origins in one of those two original branches but didn't necessarily acknowledge their lineage (and with varying levels of professionalism, training standards, and ethical practices).

And *then* there are conscious breathing practices that stem from yogic science traditions called pranayama. Pranayama is the practice of controlling your breath, but there are hundreds of different variations in the pace, volume, timing, duration, and frequency of the breath and the breath holds. Due to the popularity boom and Westernization of yoga, many yoga teachers often call pranayama breathwork.

The explosion of research into breathing has hit the mainstream with a huge range of scientific protocols for wellness through breathing practices and awareness of the nervous-system benefits, the development of the "physiological sigh" being one, which I recently saw being taught by a popular scientist on *The Tonight Show.*

Conscious breathing has gone from being something that happens in monasteries or in alternative communities to something that is now embraced by mainstream culture, and the Western medical models are jumping on board!

And it's all called breathwork!

So, it is a confusing landscape out there, and if you sign up for a breathwork class, you never know what you are going to get!

It is also important to note that this book is written referencing the style of breathwork we use at The Reconnected and can't really be generalized to all types of breathwork.

Two things are for certain:

1. Conscious breathing is in, and everyone wants to experience it!
2. The research is definitive; slower breaths through the nose that are fuller than usual will activate the parasympathetic nervous system.

To understand why we'd want to activate the parasympathetic nervous system and how it all relates to parenting and being the parent you want to be, let's explore the nervous system in detail now!

SECTION I
understanding your nervous system

CHAPTER 4

Your Nervous System —Eleanor

In this chapter, we are going to teach you how your nervous system works! This is the foundation for understanding the interconnectedness we share with our kids later in the Whole Family Nervous System section, so even if you feel like you might know this, take the time to refresh the information, because it is an important foundation.

Let's start by connecting again to why understanding the nervous system is important or even relevant for parents.

Think back to Chapter 1 for a moment and the question we asked you to consider.

We asked you to identify the most stressful or frustrating moments you have had with your kids, and then we asked you to consider, how would those moments be changed if you could authentically respond to your kids, as though they were doing the best they could in that moment?

If you could understand why they were acting the way they were and knew exactly what to do about it, those stressful moments would be pretty different, huh? Most parents say they would be able to respond the way they want to by being calmer, more patient, more playful, and less tense and worried.

Well, being able to respond like this *is what an embodied understanding of the nervous system gives you.*

So, let's get into it!

Embodied experience is at the helm!

First let's start with having a tangible experience of the polarity of the nervous system. The first step is to notice the *Current State Baseline* of your nervous system. A baseline is a starting point, a measure that reflects where you are at before you embark on practices that create change. Knowing your baseline means you can more easily track changes.

Take a moment to just notice your thoughts, feelings, body sensations. Maybe your thoughts are clear and subtle, your body warm, emotions neutral. Or maybe your mind is racing, your body tense, and your emotions slightly anxious.

Whatever you are feeling, just notice for now how you feel before the practice.

Next, notice your breathing.

Is your breath shallow or full? Does the breath come down to your belly or does it stay in your chest? Does it feel easy to breathe or hard to breathe? No right or wrong here, just noticing the quality of your breath as it is for you right now.

You don't need to change anything, just observe. These observations are your Current State Baseline for now.

Now we have two practices for you to explore the branches of the nervous system.

First, bring up your right hand to cover and block your right nostril with your thumb, and slowly breathe through your left nostril (if your left nostril blocks, just breathe slowly through both nostrils).

Pause reading and keep breathing like this for a few minutes, just long enough to feel a change in the way you are feeling.

Left-Nostril Breath

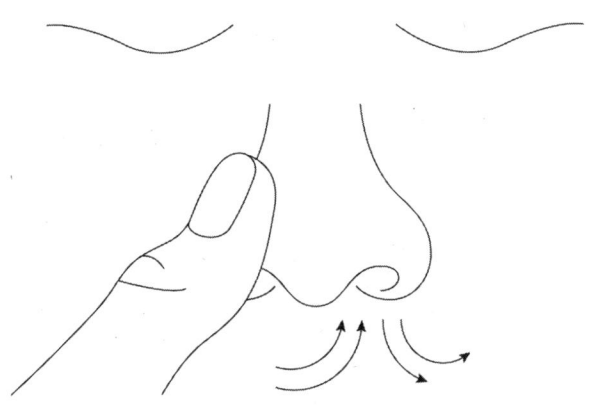

After a few minutes, let go of controlling your breath, let your hand rest back down in your lap, and spend another few moments observing your thoughts, feelings, and body sensations.

What has changed after the breathing practice? Notice and make a mental note of any subtle changes. If you would like to follow a practice video, go to www.thereconnected.com/book.

Second, let's explore the polar opposite type of breath.

Keep your hands in your lap this time, and breathe in and out through your nose, only this time, we want you to breathe in short, quick breaths.

You are rapidly breathing in and out the nose, a bit like you are running, so there is no pause between the breaths you take. Your navel will naturally pump the breath in and out. Breathe as fast as you can for just a minute or so. Again, if you would like to follow a practice video, go to www.thereconnected.com/book.

Breath of Fire

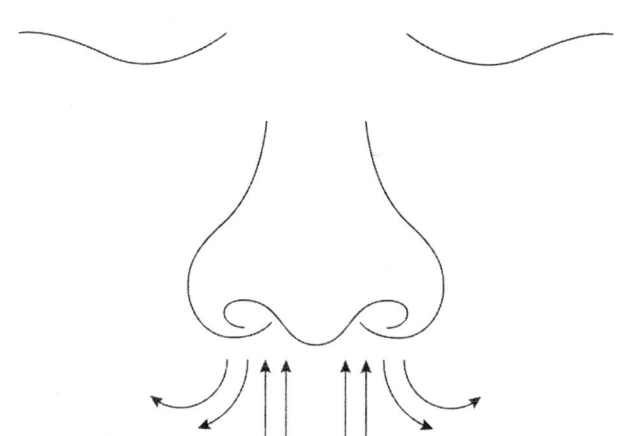

And now, let go of the practice and notice the change! How are your thoughts, feelings, and body sensations different now?

It is likely the two different ways of breathing gave you two very different experiences.

Well, this is because what you just experienced are the two different branches of the autonomic nervous system (ANS), and they have very different and complementary roles.

Let's dive into the science behind what you just experienced in your ANS.

The Autonomic Nervous System (ANS)

Scientific models of the autonomic nervous system (ANS) were first developed a little over 120 years ago by John Langley. The ANS is the part of your body that receives information from the world around you and helps you to react to your environment in ways that keep you safe. It is working all the time, tracking moment to moment what is happening around you, and is completely focused on your survival and working to keep you safe.

And it does all of this while staying in the background of your awareness.

The ANS is connected with blood pressure, breathing, metabolism, heart rate, blinking, digestion, body temperature, and more. It keeps your body in a state of balance automatically without you having to think about it.

The ANS responds to all subtle changes in the environment that require you to adjust your physiological state for your survival and well-being.

Let's say you are going for a walk, and you go out into the sun for a while, and there is a change in temperature. Your ANS will produce sweat, lower your heart rate, and make you want to sit in the shade and slow down. It does this to cool you down in response to the change in temperature. Or let's imagine it suddenly gets too cold; it will make you shiver and gasp for air in shock.

Our ANS is always trying to keep you in balance, and it does it automatically and unconsciously. And lucky! Imagine if you had to consciously regulate your temperature or intentionally digest your food! Or consciously breathe every single breath. Thank goodness that the ANS is always maintaining so much for you while we go about your life.

The ANS is also linked to your thoughts, your emotions, and your sense of connection to other people—which is why many of us have unconscious, automatic, habitual, and reactive emotions and thoughts also (especially in relationships!).

Your ANS has your best interest at heart! It is always reacting to your environment to keep you safe by responding to real and perceived threats to your safety. When a threat appears, or if you perceive you are under threat, the amygdala, the section of your brain responsible for fear, sends a signal to the hypothalamus, which stimulates the sympathetic branch of the nervous system so that you can protect yourself. Once the threat has passed, the second branch of the nervous system, the parasympathetic nervous system, calms you down and returns you to your baseline. The two branches of the ANS are designed to work in perfect tandem.

The Central Nervous System (CNS)

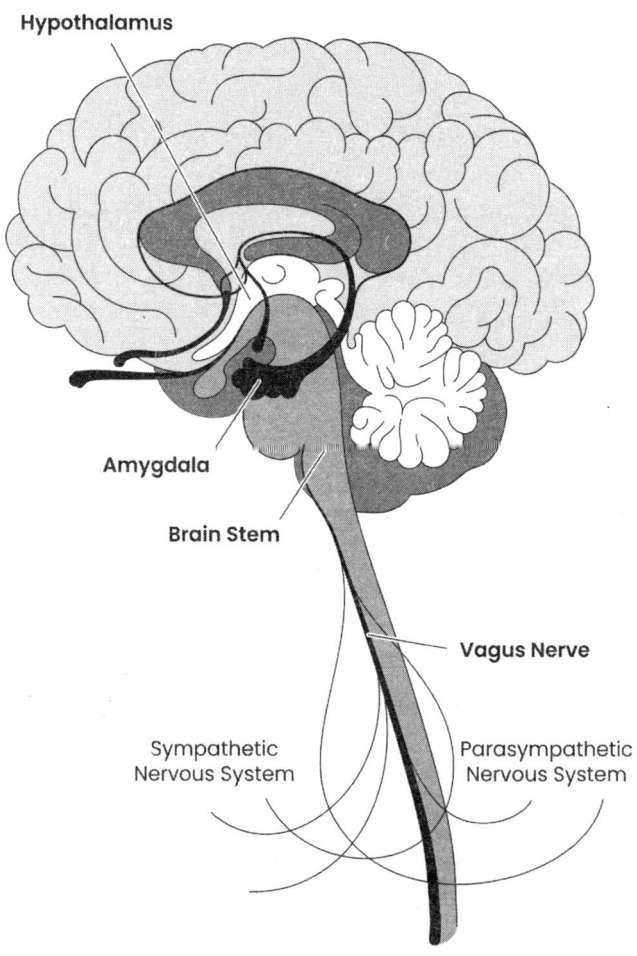

Your Nervous System—Eleanor

Let's take a break from reading information for a moment, and check in on what has been happening in your nervous system since the breathing activity we did, especially now that you have gone back to your automatic and habitual breathing while you were reading.

Think back to the fast breathing we did earlier. How did you feel? It is likely you felt hot, your thoughts were racing, and your heartbeat might have gotten faster. You might also have felt anxious or even mildly annoyed. This was your sympathetic nervous system being activated.

If you are back at the Current State Baseline you felt earlier, it means that your parasympathetic nervous system has automatically regulated you after the faster breathing exercise. When your breath returned to normal, it gave your body the message "the time to be switched on and activated is over." And you didn't need to think about this process; your body did it by itself.

Take a moment and notice if you are back at your Current State Baseline or still feeling the activation of the sympathetic nervous system. If you feel a tingling in your body, have a faster-than-usual heartbeat, or maybe you are feeling alert or your mind is going faster than usual, you are likely still in a sympathetic state.

Contrary to popular belief, sympathetic activation isn't a bad thing—it all depends on context. See, sometimes the sympathetic nervous system gets a bad rap. Because it is activated to either fight off or run away from threats. It is at work when we are angry, when we are yelling, when we feel like fighting, and when we are afraid, anxious, worried, or feel like running away, and so it tends to be associated with these less socially acceptable ways of relating to the world. It is known as the fight-or-flight response, because it helps us to mobilize to keep ourselves and others safe from threats.

Here is a real-life example of this survival response in action. I was recently at a river where lots of families were swimming, and I noticed a group of teens playing and swimming in a strong current. They were calling out playfully to each other, when suddenly, I heard a call that had an undertone of fear in it. Without thinking or planning, I stood up, started moving toward the water, took off my jumper as I walked, ready to jump in, and at the same time, I yelled out loudly to the lifeguard, "Hey, he is going under!"

Sure enough, one of the teens was struggling to stay afloat, and his friends hadn't noticed. My call alerted a lifeguard, and they swam to the rescue. A few people afterward thanked me for taking action! Well, I hadn't really thought about it. But we can say it was thanks to my sympathetic nervous system! It was my ANS's impeccable ability to detect a threat and activate the survival response that got me into action without a second thought! Before I had properly registered what was happening, I was already moving and yelling for help.

The sympathetic nervous system is also dominant at any time where we are exerting ourselves (like when we're doing exercise or athletics), during some types of positive emotions (like excitement), *as well as* in stressful or threatening situations. Reflect for a moment if you felt energized, focused, and clear while doing the fast breathing; this was the sympathetic nervous system.

Once either the threat or the excitement passes, and we are ready to switch off and calm down, our parasympathetic nervous system slows everything down again, without us needing to consciously switch ourselves off, so that we don't stay in a heightened and sympathetically activated state once it is time to relax.

The first breathing activity, left-nostril breathing, activated your parasympathetic nervous system. Perhaps you felt yourself relax a little? Think back to how it felt in your body.

Going back to the river story, the split second I saw the lifeguard moving lightning-fast through the water to the boy who needed help, I stopped mid-action and relaxed with a huge sigh of relief! The entire scenario from beginning to end probably took three seconds to unfold. Before my mind could even properly register the boy was safe, my body had already gotten the message—my senses had processed the information in a microsecond, and switched me out of survival mode. The most well-known role of the parasympathetic nervous system is to put a brake on the survival mechanisms and to relax the body after a time of stress or sympathetic activation. It slows your heart rate, slows your breath, and lets you go back to rest.

Before we go on, I am curious about something. Usually when we tell the story of the boy struggling to swim, there is someone in the audience who says something like *"I wouldn't have been able to get up to jump in the water; I can't swim well, and I would have frozen!"* I am curious—did you know, this would be the parasympathetic nervous system in action also, because it has a second important role? If you were watching the boy struggling, but your ANS made a split-second decision that even with sympathetic activation you wouldn't be able to help him to safety, then—helpful or not—the parasympathetic nervous system would immobilize and freeze you on the spot.

See, if a sympathetic response becomes ineffective, and you are unable to fight or flee, your system goes into shutdown as a survival response. You get immobilized and frozen.

Maybe you have heard of the vagus nerve; it is a part of the parasympathetic branch of the nervous system. The back of the vagus nerve is called the dorsal vagus (*dorsal* literally means "back"), and the front is called the ventral vagus (yep, *ventral* means "front").

If the first breathing practice made you feel sleepy, heavy, or like you might not be able to get up and do anything else afterward, you might have been starting to feel the dorsal vagal branch of the parasympathetic nervous system. If you cannot fight or flee your experience, then the dorsal part of the vagus nerve will create a parasympathetic overload so that you freeze and shut down. The dorsal vagal can be a challenging thing to experience; it is often connected to the emotion of shame. You might even feel a little ashamed of the *very thought* that you might have frozen rather than taken action when the boy was struggling to swim in the water. Notice how even the idea of hypothetically freezing can make us feel ashamed! It is hard at times to remember that ANS responses are not consciously chosen; they are habitual and automatic survival responses.

An immobilization of sorts also happens when we need to appease people to be safe. Let's say that someone comes up and starts yelling aggressively at you; your ANS might make the accurate decision that you cannot safely fight this person, nor can you run away. You will likely become immobilized and frozen, but playing dead is unlikely to be effective either! In this instance you might say whatever you need to say to appease them and attempt to defuse the situation. This is called fawning, or the "fawn" response.

The ventral vagus correlates to feeling safe, feeling connected, thinking clearly, having calm emotions, feeling open, and being in the present moment with the people around you. It's active in times of alert relaxation, like meditation, creative projects, and enjoyable social activities like when you're connecting deeply with another person or feeling nurtured. The ventral vagus is activated once we get clear signs of safety—not just the absence of threat.

You might remember that once the lifesaver was swimming toward the drowning teen, I stopped running instantly and took a breath out in relief. But it actually wasn't until I went back to sit with my friend who had seen the whole thing happen that I truly relaxed. We debriefed the whole thing, and I recounted a few times what had happened. As we talked, I felt even more relief, and a few times I took deep breaths as if to shake off the stress of thinking of the worst that could have happened. After a few minutes I felt completely back to myself, and we changed the topic. You see, to optimally regulate, often we need more than just the threat to pass; we need signs of safety and connection before we feel truly grounded again.

And so the ANS has five very effective ways to respond to our environment to keep us safe. The sympathetic nervous system revs us up so we can fight (attack, act, engage) or flee (run away, avoid, hide), and if these aren't going to work, the parasympathetic nervous system will overload our system and make us freeze (get stuck, immobilized, unable to speak or move) or fawn (appease, say what is needed to de-escalate a situation), and then once the threat has passed, and we are safe (*and we receive actual signs of safety, not just the removal of the threat*), we will ground back into an optimal state of arousal. If we have been in sympathetic activation, our parasympathetic nervous system is activated and we can relax into safety (the rest-and-digest response), and if we have been in a parasympathetic overwhelm (dorsal vagus), then we will likely have a boost of adrenaline and sympathetic activity to get us up and out of immobilization, and then the parasympathetic nervous system will ground us down again—the ventral vagus. This automatic, split-second perceiving and responding to our surroundings creates a constant symbiosis between us and our environment. Our body is constantly communicating with our surroundings and staying safe and balanced. The process of going into states of sympathetic activation and parasympathetic immobilization and then back into an optimal state of arousal is the process of regulation.

Ideally, in life there is always this harmonious, smooth balance between the two branches of our nervous system, a gentle collaboration that you can take for granted that allows you to go from one state to the other with constant flexibility—without thinking about it.

What is regulation?

One of the biggest myths we have been speaking out about on social media for years is that regulation means to be calm.

There is a popular message that being calm, well, it'll just fix everything.

And we see a lot of people striving to be (in their words) "regulated" or "calm" and then doing everything they can to *stay* regulated or calm in the face of everyday stressors. And in fact, with this messaging so strong on a lot of parenting social media accounts, you would be forgiven for thinking this is what we should all be striving for.

The 5 States of the Autonomic Nervous System

Hyperarousal	Optimal	Hypoarousal
Fight Flight	Ventral Vagal	Freeze Fawn

The link between "regulation" and "calm" is partly true, but not even close to the full picture.

If we look up *regulate* and *regulation* in the *Cambridge Dictionary*, the word means to "adjust something to a desired level or standard."

In the context of our nervous systems and our survival responses, the word *regulate* refers to all the physiological responses that our body goes through when adapting and surviving in the environment. Regulation is happening when our body shivers to warm us up in the cold. And yes, we are regulating when we sigh in relief when a threat has passed and our body returns to its baseline feeling of safety.

But we are also regulating when we get sympathetically activated, so we yell to get someone's attention to stay safe! We are regulating when we are adapting to the environment successfully—and by success, we mean, by staying alive!

The most widespread understanding of what regulation involves is that it is calming down after being stressed. Calming down is regulating, but it's just one aspect.

To get the full picture of the nervous system, we will introduce you to two important terms to help you understand the nervous-system stress responses and the process of regulating a little deeper.

The first is *hyperarousal*.

Hyperarousal is the fight-or-flight response, the sympathetic state when we feel fear or anger.[1] An important reminder that this is not just negative; our system is hyperaroused when we are excited (think about the kids jumping on the bed—this is hyperarousal, even though it's a ton of fun!) or when we are being active.

The second is *hypoarousal*.

When the dorsal vagus is active, we are in a hypoaroused state.[2] It can happen when we are relaxed, super chill, or stuck on our phone scrolling and can't stop! If you felt sleepy or tired when you did the left nostril breathing earlier, you might have activated the dorsal vagus and gone into a subtle parasympathetic overwhelm. Hypoarousal also happens when we get shut down, frozen, unable to move, depressed, flat, or lethargic.

When we are hyperaroused, revved up, and sympathetically activated, our nervous system will need to *down-regulate* to come back to our baseline. Your body does this automatically without thinking (just think of the way we sigh in relief after feeling afraid of something). Yet you can also consciously and deliberately practice shifting your nervous system from a sympathetic (fight-or-flight mode) to a parasympathetic (rest-and-digest mode) state by slowing down the breath. When you did the left-nostril breath, this is what you were doing!

When we are hypoaroused and feel stuck, lethargic, or down, we actually need to *up*-regulate in order to come back into balance. This usually means we need a sympathetic spike to bring ourselves up, and then we can come back to baseline. Have you noticed how kids go nuts and run around after watching TV for too long? Or maybe how you will instinctively take a short, sharp inhale to try get yourself off the couch? Again, our ANS knows exactly what to do to get us back into balance.

You can also consciously up-regulate yourself! The fast breathing you practiced earlier is a good example of a way of breathing that will give you a sympathetic boost!

So I hope you can see that the process of regulation is not just calming down; it is actually the process of moving between appropriate states of arousal, which are necessary for safe and appropriate interactions with the environment around us, and then coming back to our baseline resting state, which is ideally an optimal state of arousal, neither hyper nor hypo.

Autonomic Nervous System (ANS)

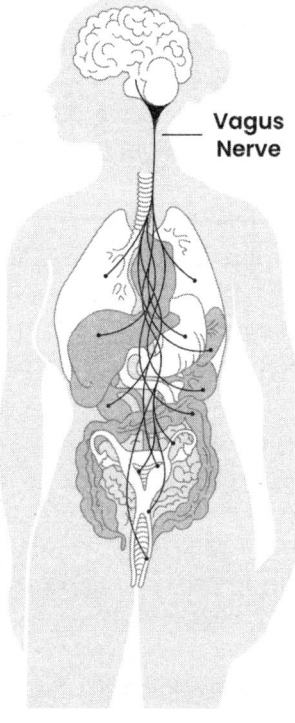

Parasympathetic Nervous System

Freeze or Fawn

- Constricts pupils
- Stimulates saliva
- Slows heartbeat
- Constricts airways
- Stimulates activity of stomach
- Inhibits release of glucose; stimulates gallbladder
- Stimulates activity of intestines
- Contracts bladder
- Promotes erection of genitals

Vagus Nerve

Sympathetic Nervous System

Flight or Fight

- Dilates pupils
- Inhibits salivation
- Increases heartbeat
- Relaxes airways
- Inhibits activity of stomach
- Stimulates release of glucose; inhibits gallbladder
- Inhibits activity of intestines
- Relaxes bladder
- Promotes ejaculation & vaginal contraction
- Secretes epinephrine & norephinephrine

When we are in an optimal state of arousal, we are in a ventral vagal state and feel balanced—both alert and relaxed—we're connected to ourselves yet available to others, we're content, we think clearly, we're positive and have perspective, and we feel safe in ourselves and the world. It is often when we feel the most ourselves.

But not everyone regulates back to ventral vagal with ease.

Now, this next part here is absolutely key, so let's just take a slower and fuller-than-usual breath together, so you can really absorb this next piece of information.

Pause a moment and take in a conscious inhalation and exhalation, slowing down the breath and breathing fuller than usual.

Okay, ready?

So the hard reality of our nervous system is that you can regulate back to ventral vagal only if you have a healthy nervous system.

Learning to use your breath in the moment is helpful because you can use it to up- or down-regulate yourself from your current state but it's a bit like a Band-Aid. Here's why.

Let's say the kids are screaming and laughing while they run around the house, and the noise starts to get to you! You are getting frustrated (sympathetic activation!). You can take a moment and slow down your breath to help yourself speak kindly to them, and the first few times it'll work.

Or you can use a more sympathetic, activating breath to get yourself up off the couch when you are stuck feeling overwhelmed and unable to face cooking dinner!

However, it doesn't stop you from getting triggered, reactive, and stressed the next time they scream or make loud sounds. You will have to slow your breath every time the sound gets too loud for you! And it doesn't help you address things like the persistent compassion fatigue and tiredness that keep us feeling lethargic and flat, sometimes from first thing in the morning!

Knowing how to up- or down-regulate your Current State is a positive, but we want to propose a potentially unpopular opinion.

Current State Influences

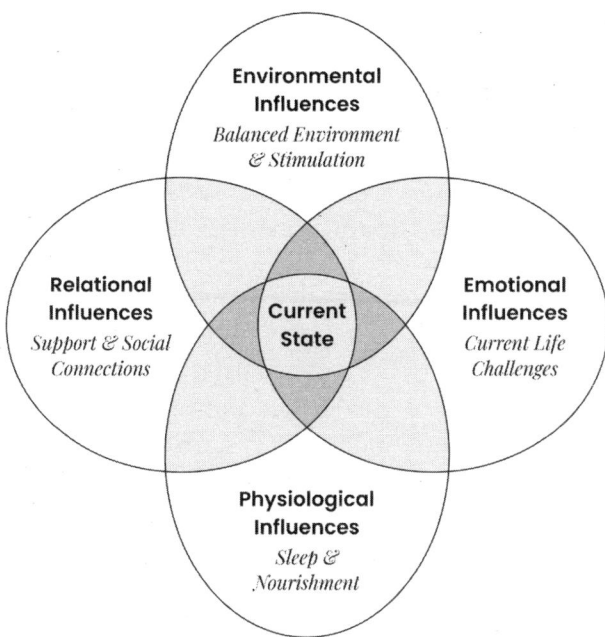

It is still a Band-Aid solution.

Of course, if you need one, using a Band-Aid is a good thing. And if you need up- or down-regulation so you can respond the way you want to in the moment when you are about to lose it, it is so helpful to have a simple tool to use.

However, knowing how to use your breath in the moment of stress doesn't help you to be able to create new ways of responding to life when the trigger happens (like when I had the paradigm shift in awareness and could suddenly respond authentically with compassion when my daughter was pushing over my son).

It doesn't change your habitual energy levels, persistent emotions, and ways of relating to the world.

For this type of change, you need to go deeper, because your nervous system doesn't just reflect what is happening at this moment in time.

Your nervous system holds the story of your entire life experience—written in your *autonomic signature*, your unique balance of sympathetic and parasympathetic activity when you are resting.

Pause. Let's take a long, slow full breath together to soak that in, and I will go into more detail in the next chapter. It is time to understand your Habitual Baseline.

CHAPTER 5

The Nervous System Holds the Imprint! —Eleanor

I was sitting in a circle of people, trying to answer the question, *"Why have you decided to come to this breathwork session today?"* and all I could say was "I am constantly stressed and triggered all the time." It was 2009, I was coming to the end of a counseling degree, I was working in community services, I was a single parent, and my kids were almost one, three, five, and six.

And life felt like total chaos.

I was alternating between feeling immense pressure and frustration in the day-to-day and completely exhausted and like I had nothing left to give. Even daily routines like getting my kids to school were highly stressful experiences for the whole family. I was so far from being the parent I wanted to be.

Like I shared in Chapter 1, I had been doing some holotropic-style breathwork, and I had a taste that transformation was possible but still wanted so much of my everyday life to change!

I had a gut feel to explore a completely different style of breathwork, with slow breathing, in and out of the nose. We started the session by reflecting on the area of life we wanted to change the most, and I shared about wanting to find parenting easier. During the breath session, I experienced lots of body sensations, some old memories that seemed pretty random were just moving through my mind's eye, and subtle emotions like guilt and regret came up. Compared to my previous experiences, this breathwork felt really subtle, and while I enjoyed it, I went back to life not really expecting much had changed.

I was still under the impression that I needed to have a huge cathartic aha moment to change my life.

A month later, when I went back for a second session, the facilitator asked me how I was doing at school drop-off and how triggered I was feeling in the day-to-day. And I said, "School drop-offs haven't ever really been an issue." I remember feeling confused by why she was asking! Over the month, the way I was relating to life had changed so much I had forgotten that I had ever been struggling!

It wasn't until the facilitator reminded me that I had shared just a month ago about being triggered "one hundred percent of the time" that I realized just how much I had changed at a day-to-day level!

I felt so different in my body just a few weeks later.

I didn't know it then, but I had a new *Habitual Baseline* in my nervous system.

I was amazed that change that would normally take a long time in counseling through goal setting, exploring triggers, planning changes, practicing, reflecting, then coming back for a second session to review how it went, then going back to try again . . . instead seemed to come from my body, creating space for me to authentically do things differently, without any effort.

The philosophy behind this more subtle and relaxed way of breathing is that it allows you to take an integrated step toward releasing whatever is in the way of the change you are ready to embody in life. I was experiencing integration. Integration occurs when the root cause of stress or trauma no longer impacts our present moment, and the most common sign of integration is forgetting that we ever had an issue!

I was obsessed.

For years I dedicated myself to using this gentler style of breathwork to positively influence my daily life. Simple but big things started to shift for me. For example, I had always been pretty shy! When I was at a mothers' group, I would literally hide behind my kids and wait for them to connect with a child, and *then* I would speak to their parents. I could spend an entire social event feeling frozen and just grateful I had the kids to preoccupy me. Now I speak to large groups of people with no worries and never describe myself as shy at all.

The improvements in my overall well-being felt mind-blowing.

I was thriving rather than surviving.

During my early days as a counselor at a local community center, I noticed something striking. Working with clients who did both talk therapy and breathwork showed me two very different paths to change. In breathwork sessions, people's behaviors would shift between one session and the next. These weren't forced changes—they just happened, almost like magic. Someone would come back saying, "I don't know what happened, but I just started responding differently to my kids."

Talk therapy was different.

Sure, people made progress, but it was slow. They'd gain excellent insights about their patterns and understand exactly why they were getting triggered. But turning that understanding into real change? That took tons of practice, willpower, and constant reminders of how to "do it differently next time." I rarely saw someone make the same kind of spontaneous shifts through talking that I saw happen regularly through working with the breath. While talk therapy helped people understand themselves better, it usually stayed at that intellectual level—knowing what to do but having to work really hard to actually do it.

Change never really landed in the body through talking.

In fact, many breathwork participants would say after a breathwork session, "I could never have realized this through talking!"

I was fascinated by how conscious breathing and deep connection to our somatic experience could have such an incredible power to integrate and transform the way we do life, so much so that our own minds have to catch up with the new ways we could do things!

It felt like I was mostly living in two worlds: on weekends I ran breathwork workshops, and during the week I delivered strictly evidence-based talk therapies, and the two felt like they would never cross over.

Years later, in the mid 2000s, the counseling team went to a conference with an incredible lineup: Gabor Maté, Dr. Daniel Siegel, Stephen Porges, Bessel van der Kolk, Dan Hughes, and more. Suddenly there was an evidence base for why the body should be included when we are doing counseling work! It was my first experience of the previously separate worlds of breathwork and counseling and therapy coming into the same space.

The science of neurobiology had entered my sphere!

Not long after, as a psychology student, I was due to complete a yearlong study for an honors thesis. This opened the door for me to explore in depth what I'd been witnessing in practice. I immersed myself in research about the nervous system, trauma, mindfulness, breath, and somatic therapies. A few key findings emerged:

- Our nervous system connects to virtually every aspect of our well-being.
- The breath, through the vagus nerve, offers a direct path to influence our nervous system.

The Nervous System Holds the Imprint!—Eleanor

While exciting, the research left me with a puzzle. Studies showed:

- Breathing practices could shift nervous-system function in minutes.
- Better nervous-system function is linked to fewer depression, anxiety, and PTSD symptoms, and increased well-being.

But something was missing. Most studies looked only at immediate, short-term changes—how breathing affected the nervous system in one session. They weren't capturing the profound, lasting shifts I'd seen in my clinical work, where people spontaneously began responding differently to life without conscious effort. The research suggested there were connections between breath, nervous system, and well-being. But it wasn't yet explaining how conscious breathing could create such deep, sustainable transformations in people's lives.

And it especially did not go near explaining how things like Core Beliefs, self-perception, and long-term relationship patterns could change so dramatically using gentle, conscious breathing. I wanted to understand how the breath could integrate so much!

I knew that neurobiology held more answers; I just needed to find them.

My breathwork teacher had told me that when we are little, our beliefs about life get locked into our body via our breath, and therefore they can be released through our breath.[1]

The breathwork theory is that we unconsciously use our breath to suppress negative or limiting experiences so we can cope with the hard things that have happened. Just think of the way we gasp in shock when we get a fright, or how often our breathing is shallow when we are feeling down or stressed. Limiting experiences are said to be stored in our breath, which is why conscious breathing practices can access these unprocessed emotions and experiences and release them so that they are no longer impacting us.

I was theorizing that the nervous system is where stress and trauma are "locked in," and because the breath is the quickest doorway to the nervous system, it is also why the breath could be used to integrate stress from the past. Either that, or maybe as someone's overall nervous system improves, there is a natural correlation in improvement across all the areas that are linked to nervous-system functioning. Seems simple and obvious right? But at the time, it was hard to find support for this in the literature.

One day when I was trying to explain all of this to the professor overseeing my research, he said to me, "I think you might be interested in looking at a person's *'at rest'* baseline of nervous-system functioning."

I was intrigued . . . and took another dive into reading.

You will remember that a baseline is a starting point to use as a comparison when measuring change. And as you would expect, the Resting Baseline of the nervous system refers to the activity in the ANS when we are resting. It is our default state of being when we are under no stress or pressure. It makes sense that when we are at rest and in a safe environment, ideally the ANS should be completely out of survival mode, in an optimal state of arousal (high in parasympathetic activity), present, calm yet alert, secure, safe, playful, self-connected, and available to others for connection.

I found a lot of research that showed people who have high levels of sympathetic nervous-system activity when they are at rest often also have symptoms of depression[2] and anxiety.[3,4] It seems that when someone is living with trauma or a mood disorder, their nervous system is rarely in a parasympathetic state, even when they are at rest. Their baseline stress levels are high regardless of what is happening around them. It makes sense to me that this is the result of unintegrated past traumatic experiences, or the weight of persistent patterns of worry and negative rumination.

I had seen this in the counseling room with kids and families who had experienced trauma and had a felt sense of it with my own experiences with PTSD, where even though no real threat was present, every moment was impacted emotionally, mentally, and physically by threats from the past. Even when people know they are logically safe, they might still startle easily, be jumpy and scared, or be stuck in an emotionally flat and frozen state. With trauma, the nervous system stays in survival mode and relates to the moment as if the threat is still present and happening now.

But what if you're not necessarily clinically depressed or recovering from PTSD? Can you still have a high level of stress stored in your body?

Let's think about a stressful or adverse experience that is more like a "little *t* trauma," which are the experiences that impact you, like parents divorcing, financial pressure, or not fitting in at school, but they do not necessarily cause PTSD. Like having a bad experience with a dog when you are little and then still feeling tense and jumpy around them as adults—the stress response is locked in.

These findings mirrored the breathwork philosophy that unconsciously held stressful experiences from when we were little and impact our present moment until we resolve them as adults. We will go into this in more detail in Section II, Understanding Your Child's Nervous System, but for now, just be open to the idea that the experiences we can remember as an adult are the tip of the iceberg of what is held in our nervous system, and that all of these experiences can be stored up and are reflected in our at-rest baseline functioning!

It seems that stress can snowball!

When small but stressful things happen over and over, it becomes harder and harder for the parasympathetic nervous system to override and halt the stress responses. Basically, this means it becomes harder and harder for the body to come back to the optimal arousal state of ventral vagal after a stressor. Over time, if we don't resolve or let go of things, then eventually, even when we are at rest, we are in a degree of survival mode.

I began to hypothesize that in breathwork we were Releasing the stored stress from past experiences from our nervous system, meaning our at-rest Parasympathetic Baseline would increase over time, as the impact of the past became integrated.

I began to create a rather ambitious study for a yearlong honors project. I took 20 participants and met them for breathwork sessions three times a week for six weeks, with the goal of understanding the impact on their At-Rest Baseline and a few other areas of well-being (cognition, anxiety, and social behavior). I modified the breathwork I had been trained in to align even more with what the literature suggested was to activate the parasympathetic nervous system (more on this in Chapter 9).

The results suggested that the hunches I was having were likely on track, with all participants showing a higher Parasympathetic Baseline after the six weeks of breathwork. The small size of the group meant any firm conclusions were limited, although the results showed the value of continuing to research the topic, and this is exactly what has happened since then! Out of curiosity, I did a quick Google Scholar search with the keywords *parasympathetic* and *breathing* and found 20,000 studies between 2017 and 2023, more than double the amount as 10 years prior! This includes a number of meta-analyses exploring the effect of slower-than-usual breathing on stress, the vast majority of studies finding that slow, full, nasal breathing activates the parasympathetic nervous system and has a wide range of benefits.[5] It will be a very interesting decade ahead as the evidence becomes more conclusive—there is more to explore!

Discover Your Baseline

Before we keep going, we want to remind you that sympathetic activity and ANS stress responses are functional and important. Even the natural autonomic physiology of one breath reflects this: our sympathetic nervous system is active when we inhale, and the parasympathetic is active when we exhale.[6] They are complementary, and one cannot exist without the other. Both branches of the nervous system are necessary, and avoiding states of sympathetic activation or dysregulation is as unnecessary, unrealistic, and impossible as avoiding difficult feelings in life.

Optimal functioning means we should be responsive to our environment—within the context of what is happening around us—and then return to ventral vagal when it is time to rest. When we have a high Parasympathetic Baseline, we are increasingly safe to feel all our emotions, and we can ride out states of dysregulation, knowing it is to be felt and will pass. We can feel big feelings and ground down afterward. When the autonomic nervous system is healthy, it's very flexible; it changes easily in response to what is happening around us, reacting to stresses or activating us to get things done and then calming down again lots of times throughout the day.

When we're constantly stressed or anxious or nervous or going through a lot in life, we have less-flexible responses to the world, our nervous system becomes more rigid, and there is less of a difference between an autonomic stress response and resting. The issue is not that we have gotten dysregulated; it is that we haven't grounded down afterward. We feel stressed, and we stay stressed. We are stuck in the past at the level of the nervous system, so true rest and relaxation becomes unachievable or limited—this is the problem. Our nervous system is not in context to what is happening around us anymore.

Are you beginning to see why we say at The Reconnected "your nervous system holds the story of your entire life experience"?

This unintegrated stress from the past is reflected in our Habitual Baseline.

Habitual Baseline

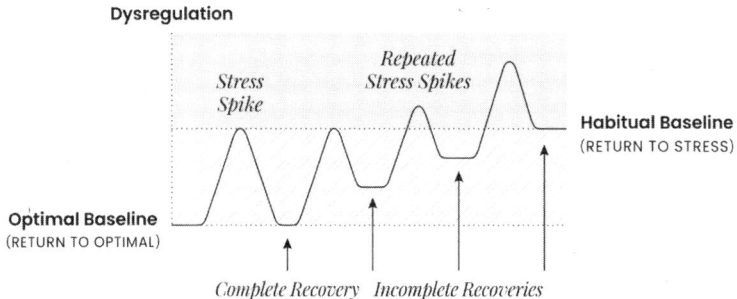

Okay, let's pause, take a deep breath, and reflect.

Who here is having some ahas reading this and recognizing that you might not be returning to a ventral vagal state? That your Habitual Baseline is high in stress? Every time we teach this content, a large part of the audience identifies as being stuck in hypo- or hyperarousal, and some people even say they cannot remember ever being in a ventral vagal state!

Ventral vagal is an optimal state of arousal when we are alert yet relaxed, we feel available for connection, and we are full of energy but also grounded.

When you are in ventral vagal:
Your body feels both relaxed *and* energized.
Your breathing is full and easy, without you trying.
You're present but not vigilant.
The world feels naturally interesting, not threatening.
You can just *be*, without effort.

While our Habitual Baseline might keep us stuck in subtle survival mode, it doesn't have to stay that way. What we're really after is what we call a Reconnected Baseline—a resting ventral vagal state.

Reconnected Baseline

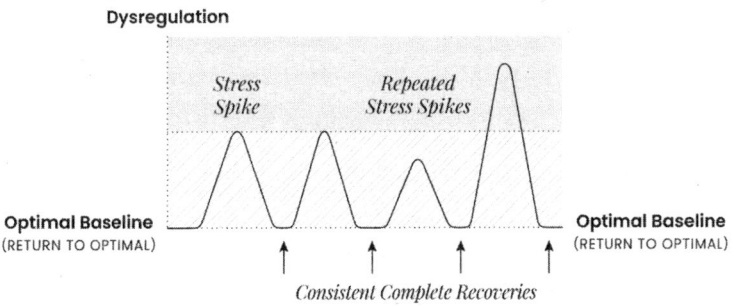

Think of it like this: Your Habitual Baseline is where you're starting from—perhaps stuck in patterns of stress, reactivity, or shutdown. Your Reconnected Baseline is where your system naturally wants to be: flexible, resilient, energized, and connected to yourself.

This isn't about forcing yourself to be calm; it's about releasing stored patterns and allowing your system to remember its natural state. When you understand this, the goal becomes clear: not just managing your Current State Baseline, but gradually shifting where you naturally return to when you are at rest.

Reconnecting to Your Authentic Self

Being able to regulate back to a Reconnected Baseline is like coming home to ourselves. Over weeks and months of working with the nervous system, we begin to have glimpses of a different way of being. At first, these moments might be brief: a morning where we naturally wake feeling refreshed, a challenging situation where we are proud of our response.

Layer by layer, these experiences build.

People start noticing subtle but significant shifts: *"I feel more like myself than ever"* or *"I'm remembering who I am beneath all the stress."* It's not that stress or emotions disappear—rather, we begin to recognize them as experiences moving through us, not who we are at our core.

The beauty of this process is that we're not becoming someone new; we're gradually rediscovering our natural state. The peace within, the playfulness within, the compassion within—these qualities emerge not through effort but through removing the layers of protection we've built up over time. Each return to the ventral vagal state becomes a reconnecting affirmation, *"Ah yes, this is who I really am."*

Reflecting on Your Baseline

When you are at rest, what is your Habitual Baseline?

When you are resting at the end of the day, ready to switch off, what do you experience? Are you in a hyper- or hypoaroused state?

Hyperaroused Baseline:

- Mind constantly scanning for what needs to be done
- Can't fully relax even when everything's fine
- Quick to startle or feel irritated
- Body often feels "tired but wired"
- Might pride yourself on being productive
- Subtle anxiety at all times

Hypoaroused Baseline:

- Often feeling flat or lacking energy
- Get stuck scrolling on the phone for long periods, unable to stop
- Can zone out or dissociate easily
- Might feel heavy or weighed down
- Hard to get motivated or excited
- Could sleep for hours but never feel refreshed
- Social interactions feel draining
- Often feel "stuck" or "numb"

How often do you return to ventral vagal? Do you experience the Reconnected Baseline?

Why is this important? Your Nervous-System Baseline determines how you handle life's biggest challenges. I saw this clearly while counseling bushfire survivors in 2012. All had fled with just the clothes on their backs; all faced initial trauma and shock. But their recovery paths differed dramatically based on their existing baseline.

Those with strong Ventral Vagal Baseline indicators (positive mental health, strong social networks, positive sense of self) before the fires typically bounced back within weeks or months. Others, whose systems were already stressed, often needed years to recover. When your baseline is anchored in the ventral vagus, you can weather major storms—you'll still feel the impact, but you bounce back.

A second powerful example of this emerged after the 2022 floods in our hometown. One participant in our 21-Day Nervous System Reset (a program designed to bring you back to a Reconnected Baseline) had lost everything in the floods. Their message after their home was lost stunned us:

"If this had happened a few months ago, it would have been the end of me—even small issues felt overwhelming. Now, strangely, I can handle it. I'm there for my kids and thriving despite losing everything. I'm actually coping better now than I was before, when life was easier."

This is the power of a Reconnected Baseline: not avoiding difficulty but having the resilience to move through it with strength.

In the next few chapters, you will discover a lot about your own unique ANS, your baseline, and what it says about your overall life experience. In many ways, your nervous system and your unique at-rest autonomic signature—your personal state of hyper-, hypo-, and optimal arousal while you are at rest—really does tell the story of your entire life experience.

So, how do you know what old stories and experiences you are carrying in your nervous system that are influencing your Habitual Baseline? It's easier than you'd think. The signs are often right in front of you, especially if you have kids!

CHAPTER 6

Parenting, Why Is It So Challenging?—Emma

Picture this: you're having what feels like a perfectly normal morning. The kids are playing, you're getting things done, everything seems fine. Then suddenly—maybe it's a certain whiny tone in your child's voice or the sound of siblings fighting upstairs or perhaps just the way your toddler looks at you while deliberately dropping their food on the floor—and something in you snaps. In an instant, your heart races, your jaw clenches, and you suddenly feel tense and overwhelmed. You are hyperaroused!

Sound familiar?

Let me share my own journey of discovering the stories and stress within my Habitual Baseline.

I was raised in a home with a lot of dysregulation. Life at home was chaotic: My mum worked really long hours, and I spent a lot of time with my dad, who was carrying some pretty intense war trauma and had quite a serious drinking problem. By the time I was a young adult, I was living in a constant state of anxiety. I had moved out of my parents' home at age 16, after being spotted by a modeling agent. I was whisked off to London from my small hometown in Australia to work with an agency, walking all the big fashion weeks and booking editorials in magazines like *Vogue*, *Harper's Bazaar*, and *Cosmopolitan*.

I was living an incredible life in many ways, but I was in a state of stress, and my personal life was chaotic. From the outside it looked like my life was a dream. I was successful, making great money, and traveling, but I was also having panic attacks about simple things and barely coping with adult life. I remember one day being absolutely stuck in freeze mode at an ATM machine after it ate my EFTPOS card; my hands cramped up, I was short of breath, and I was absolutely frozen in panic. It wasn't even a big deal; I was outside the bank and could go inside to ask them to help, but I was a mess of anxiety and was not functioning rationally at all.

My Habitual Baseline was high in sympathetic activity, and while I didn't know anything about the nervous system, I did know something was wrong. I even went to the doctor, but he said, "You've just got something called anxiety; you'll probably have it your whole life, and here is a prescription that can help you," aka Valium. So I thought it was normal or just a random mental illness, because no one was mentioning how I may be carrying a lot of unintegrated stress from my childhood.

So, how *do* we know what we are carrying in our nervous system and what is contributing to our Habitual Baselines of resting stress?

For most people, awareness comes once we get to a place where we are in pain enough that we have no choice but to face reality, or when we commit to something really important to us and it requires us to evolve past old ways of doing things. In moments like these, we are motivated or even simply have no choice but to dig deep and reflect on how we really feel about our lives.

When we want to know what unintegrated stressors we are carrying, we don't have far to look; the answers are often right in front of us, in the triggers and reactions we experience every day!

Parenting, Why Is It So Challenging?—Emma

When my panic attacks became more regular and debilitating, I finally saw how stressed I was. I was in enough pain to change! But when I look back, the signs of suppressed emotions were there for a long time before that. I had known for most of my early adult years that I was not good at expressing my emotions. Friends would say I was "strong," and boyfriends would say I was "cold" when I couldn't be emotional in a fight. If there was an emotional conversation, I would shut down and cut them off from the conversation by walking away, leaving the room, or I would just freeze, go blank, and not know what to say. I remember after one argument I had with a boyfriend, I wondered if there was something wrong with me, because I felt numb and shut off, and I just couldn't cry!

I kept thinking, *"Why can't I cry? I just want to cry! This is so painful,"* and then one day (during a breathwork session) it all clicked. I could hear my dad saying to me, "Don't cry" over and over and over again. He'd say this every single time I'd become emotional; if I fell over and was hurt, he'd be there with me but say, "Don't cry. Just stop crying, and I'll help you."

When I was a young adult, I called my dad for help with a stressful situation. As I was mumbling in tears on the phone, he just kept saying, "Stop crying. Stop, and we'll sort it out." This realization was a huge aha for me. I had never been allowed to cry, and so I just absolutely numbed out in the face of other people's emotions, and in situations where I was emotional, I disconnected rather than felt things.

When I was little, I had to shut down when I had big feelings.

So, when big feelings happened as an adult, my nervous system would go into shutdown—hypoarousal!

I could watch it happen, but there was no way I could make myself feel or stay connected to people in these moments. Have you ever noticed how there are specific situations, or things that other people do or say, that we find hard to tolerate and are then unable to choose the way we respond?

For me, I really did *want* to feel the emotions, and I would have loved to cry and to be there for other people when they were upset, but I just couldn't. Whenever other people were emotional, or even if I started to get emotional, I just shut down, and there was nothing I could do about it! Then there came a time when I couldn't hold it in anymore!

Everyone has their own things that they find stressful, depending on their life experiences.

Maybe you have specific emotions that feel intolerable or that you feel embarrassed about. It could be a negative emotion like anger, but it could also be joy or excitement. Or maybe there is a certain look that your partner or kids give you that makes you furious. Or a tone of voice one of your siblings uses that still makes you feel tiny and like you want to disappear.

These moments of being triggered are doorways to the past that show you exactly what you have had to suppress and store in your nervous system.

What is a trigger?

A trigger is something that activates a reaction from the past. Triggers can be external things, like situations, other people's behaviors, or anything else that is happening around us, and they can be internal experiences like physical sensations, emotions, thoughts, or memories. For example, your child might come and sit next to you for a cuddle; the sensation of their skin touching yours suddenly makes you feel absolutely suffocated! It comes out of nowhere, and it's all you can do to reciprocate the affection. Or maybe there is an external trigger—your kids start screaming with joy. You are instantly tense and overwhelmed—you want to shut it down! In both situations, the reaction is most likely out of context to the circumstance that triggered it.

Reactions and Reactivity

Let's think about reactions and reactivity.

When we are reactive, we feel out of control of our response, and we often regret the way we think, feel, or behave in those moments. We feel out of our own control, and like we have little choice about the way we behave. We might be unconsciously reactive, or we might watch ourselves react while simultaneously wishing we could stop or rewind what we are saying. Most commonly, though, reactions are automatic, habitual, and unconscious.

When we are in a reactive state, we are usually either hypoaroused or hyperaroused and in an active state of dysregulation.

Do you recall how the ANS system changes our physiology to keep us safe without us even thinking about it? It governs our unconscious, automatic survival responses, like making sure our heart is beating and that we are breathing. Thank goodness we don't have to think about these things! Remember how this automatic, instinctual part of us is essential for our survival because it helps us make split-second decisions?

When we are triggered, emotional reactions and thought patterns also happen without us consciously deciding to respond that way.

This is the ANS at work again!

No one ever really consciously chooses to get angry when the kids are too noisy or to shut down when our kids are crying. It just happens!

Reactions are automatic, unconscious, habitual ways of relating to the world that are stored in our nervous system and are reactivated when a situation or emotion in the present closely resembles or feels similar to something we have been unsafe to feel previously. Our ANS is always trying to keep us safe.

What are your triggers?

For this next section, it will help if you can bring a trigger and a reaction to mind. Think of the things that your kids or partner do that you cannot handle. The things that bring out the worst in you, when no matter how hard you try, you cannot be the person you want to be in that moment. What is happening around you or within you that triggers the reaction?

And now what is the reaction?

How do you feel, what do you think, and what do you do? (Don't hold back here! Let's get to the good, the bad, and the parts of ourselves we'd rather not see—it's the only way to grow!)

Now what type of nervous-system activation happens when you are reacting? Do you get into a hypo- or hyperaroused state? Meaning, do you get defeated, flat, and overwhelmed (hypo) or anxious, angry, and revved up (hyper)?

Now, if you find it hard to think of a specific trigger or reaction . . . quick question: Could it be that you are blaming other people for the way you feel, think, and behave at times?

The hard truth is, we can never grow in an area we don't take responsibility for our reaction in. This does not mean our reactions are not understandable, nor does it diminish hardship, challenges, and the reality that most parents are parenting without the support they really need. However, without taking responsibility for our reactions, we can't cultivate an attitude that is supportive for gaining self-awareness and regulation.

Sometimes, when we cannot identify an area where we are triggered, it is because we are blaming other people for our reactions. For example, for the longest time I used to feel so explosive in the car if the kids would fight while we were driving. In fact, once when my son was a baby and he was crying, I had a small car accident! The sound and the distractions made me tense up, my mind started racing, and I would yell at everyone to be quiet, even though I knew they were all just needing to let off some steam too! I never realized loud noises in the car were a trigger for me because I honestly thought, *"They should not be so loud while I am driving."* I felt so justified in my reaction.

Now, I actually do think my reaction was completely understandable! It was loud, the kids were little, and it was really, really hard to concentrate. All true and valid.

But the thing with blame is, it also keeps us stuck because we feel so justified. We can then cling to our reaction so we are in the right, and I sometimes think we subtly expect that our reactions should be reason enough for other people to change, which means we avoid the need to explore our reaction.

Blame is the old paradigm of relating.

The new paradigm is personal responsibility.

You have to yell at the kids in the car only a few times to know that even if it's understandable that you lose it, it rarely does anything productive, and you tend to feel much worse and possibly spiral down in guilt as a result of being less than the parent you want to be. If anything, once we have lost it, we tend to blame others even more to avoid the shame of owning the reactions that we aren't proud of!

I remember the day when I realized that my reaction to noise in the car was actually a trigger! Phew, it was such a relief to bring some curiosity and space so I could start to be open to understanding why I was responding the way I did rather than being stuck in justifying myself and the reactions I hated being stuck in!

So, dig a little deeper, and even if you can't think of something that you think would count as a trigger, try and find a moment when you are not proud of your parenting, and think about what is happening around you when you feel that way.

Maybe it is bedtime, or if you've just sat down with a cup of tea and you get interrupted, or when the kids fight, or perhaps you hate whining . . . whatever it is, find that one thing that really gets under your skin. That is your trigger, and then think about how you feel, think, and behave, and that is your reaction.

Why is parenting so challenging?

Parenting is challenging because ultimately, it is triggering.

It is true and valid that parenting is hard. It's emotionally and physically taxing, no matter how much you love being a parent. In particular, the way that many parents are alone with their kids for many hours or feel financial pressure or the expectation to do all the things alongside parenting—career, relationships, health, personal growth, and the list goes on. The dysregulation of parents who are isolated, unsupported, and raising kids during stressful times could be seen as a healthy reaction to an unhealthy society in many ways.

But ultimately the hardest part of being a parent is that our kids trigger us.

We can't give what we didn't get

The hardest reality of being a parent is that we cannot give to our children what we did not receive ourselves. Well, actually, the main problem with parenting is we do not realize this is what is happening, and instead we are stuck feeling angry, annoyed, or avoidant and overwhelmed by our kids' needs and their emotional expressions with no idea what is driving these reactions. And all of us have grown up with some level of emotional suppression.

For example, many of our parents thought that if we stop crying, then we will feel better! In fact, crying is a way for our body to release emotional stress, and if we are not able to cry, we store this stress in our bodies.

When we have to suppress, deny, or inhibit a need or an emotion, it does not go away. Instead, we develop coping mechanisms that act to keep the emotion pushed away. Why would our physiology do this, if it is so bad for us? Well, when we are little, helpless, and dependent, we have very little choice. We need our parents' acceptance, connection, and care to survive, and so we have to abandon ourselves, our needs, and our emotions so as to survive. Again, it's a survival response we have, thanks to our ANS. Parenting becomes challenging because we are stuck between aspiring to be the best parent we can be, to give our children everything that they need, and then we are held back by the parts of ourselves that remain suppressed or inhibited by coping mechanisms. Usually, this stuckness, especially when we know better but cannot do better, means we are coming from an unintegrated part of ourselves.

If your Habitual Baseline is high in stress, you might be triggered or activated a lot of the time. Small things will feel like big things. You may not switch off at the end of the day, or you can't relax even when the kids are playing happily.

Habitual Baseline *(with Triggers)*

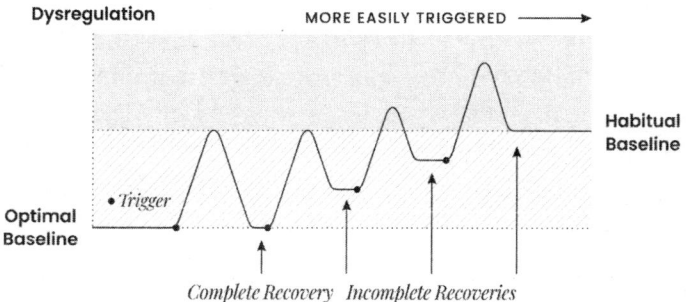

Complete Recovery   Incomplete Recoveries

If you have a Reconnected Baseline, you will feel able to rest when it is appropriate, and when triggered, you will be safe to feel and validate your emotions yet free to choose your response and ground down afterward. This choice will come from an authentic space, and you might even have moments of noticing just how differently you can respond rather than react at times that used to be stressful.

Reconnected Baseline *(with Triggers)*

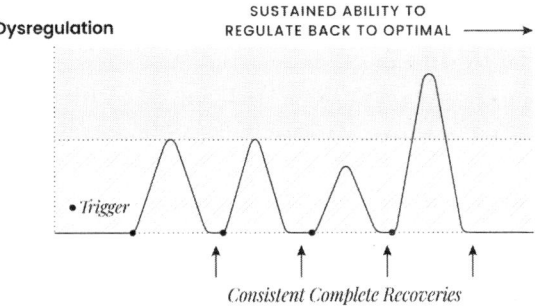

Luckily, there are ways you can integrate stressors and get back to a Reconnected Baseline so that when we do get triggered, we do have the space to respond the way we want to. We have found that the first step toward a Reconnected Baseline is understanding the five Stress Archetypes that show us what nervous-system state is your go-to when you are triggered and/or stressed.

CHAPTER 7

The Five Stress Archetypes—Emma

Have you noticed that when you are triggered or reactive you have a set of "go-to" reactions?

That when you experience a certain trigger, your reaction is often the same? Maybe your reaction escalates a bit each time, but the feeling of being triggered is very familiar.

Very often we have repeated patterns of reacting, and we experience the same set of emotions, feelings, and behaviors over and over in life. That is why when people find The Reconnected, they are often despairing about specific things that they feel really fed up about and are struggling to change, like not being able to stop yelling, or staying busy so they never have to stop, or never being able to feel playful.

We have also noticed that when people get triggered, most experience one of five reactions, which we call the Five Stress Archetypes. We have found that it can be very helpful to identify which archetype we most relate to. It is the first step to creating the space you need to respond rather than reacting during moments that normally feel stressful.

So, in this chapter, we will explore the Five Stress Archetypes in detail. The first (and most common) one is the Yeller.

The Yeller: Fight Response

Hands up if you have already lost your temper with your kids today?

So many parents are distraught about losing their temper with their kids. Many parents, after yelling or losing their cool, end up in a spiral of shame, awake in bed at night wracked with guilt, promising themselves they'll do it differently tomorrow but then winding up feeling like a failure when the rush of anger hits them again in the morning.

For someone stuck in a dysregulated "Fight" response, the struggle with anger is *that* real.

When we first met Tessa, she was in a really challenging time in her life. Her marriage was ending, and her family was separating. She was suddenly a solo mum with two young, big-energy kids. After a lot of drama in the lead-up to her marriage dissolving, she realized she had been chronically stressed for a long time.

The only clue was her smartwatch that could read her heart rate. The reader would constantly show her in the red zone, which meant her body was stressed, but she kept thinking she was fine because she was so used to operating at that level that it felt normal. Tessa found herself going from 0 to 100 when the smallest thing happened with her kids. She would think she was relatively calm, but then something would happen, and she would suddenly find herself yelling at her kids and wonder where it would come from and why that was happening. She was explosive, even though she didn't want to be.

When you're in a Fight response, you:

- Feel tense, frustrated, and snappy.
- Get angry and yell.

- Go from 0 to 100 and explode.
- Can be controlling and demanding.
- Might feel like you're constantly gritting your teeth or swallowing mean words.

When your Habitual Baseline is stuck in the Yeller, you *more often than not*:

- Have a low level of frustration all the time about small things.
- Feel like your kids or others are against you.
- Have to work hard not to be rough when your kids are angry.
- Feel like you want to hit, kick, throw, or punch.
- Feel powerless against rage.
- Wake up feeling exhausted from managing anger.

If you're stuck in the sympathetic activation that is the Fight response, after the hyperaroused state has passed, there can be a lot of shame associated with losing your temper. For Tessa, it was when she saw her kids starting to also yell at each other, and she knew she had to do something about the pattern she was in. That was when she found The Reconnected.

The thing is, it is possible to befriend anger. Anger is an important and powerful messenger when we have an integrated relationship with it. When the Yeller creates the inner space, the fight response can be felt, acknowledged, and then grounded in a safe and integrated way.

When you have integrated the Yeller, you can:

- Use your anger to powerfully create boundaries.
- Feel safe with anger and know how to express it in a way that keeps everyone safe.
- Recognize that anger has a message or reflects an unmet need.
- Over time, learn to communicate and get your needs met before you're angry.

The Gifts of the Yeller

Imagine having a healthy relationship with anger where it becomes a signpost for where you have stepped away from your commitment to yourself, your values, your purpose, your passion, or the activities that bring you more energy and vibrancy. This is the gift of integrating the Yeller archetype. Your anger has a sacred message for you—when you are safe to feel it, you can hear it.

After breathwork, Tessa landed in a place where she recognizes her stress-response patterns. She has been able to step outside of the victim mindset she used to struggle with and now approaches hard moments from a place of curiosity about how she is showing up, especially when things aren't working out the way she wants them to.

"I'm feeling more joy. I'm actually tapping into how I'm feeling; I'm not down all the time. I'm able to sit with emotions and allow them to be there to release them but not be so swept up in it. And now to be on the other side of that, where everything's possible and life's so expansive, and everything that I'm wanting and needing in life is dropping in . . . it's just so incredible."

The Mantra for the Yeller

My anger is telling me something important. I alchemize anger to create boundaries and know it as a creative force. My anger is protective, and I express it freely.

The Hustler: Flight Response

Shelby had a 10-month-old and 3-year-old daughter when she found The Reconnected. She was living in Australia after growing up in America, so she was far away from her family, and she was on maternity leave and feeling stressed about having to go back to work as a yoga teacher.

She had been experiencing issues with her sleep. She'd get a sense of doom when bedtime was approaching, and it was a constant battle, because when she couldn't get enough sleep, it really affected her ability to look after herself, and then parenting was really hard! She began to rely on having a glass of wine, or up to three or more, as a way to calm herself down in the evenings, but she felt it was fine, especially since it's accepted as part of "mommy wine" culture. Before she knew it, she found herself having a drink every night and knew that wasn't healthy or who she wanted to be, but she could not see a way out. She knew drinking was a way to self-soothe as a little temporary escape from the pain she was feeling, but she didn't know another way.

Shelby felt disconnected from her eldest daughter at the time, and she didn't know how to fix the connection with her. If her older daughter pushed over the younger one, she'd snap at her and then find herself wanting to run away. When her daughter had a meltdown, she'd have the urge to just escape, and at her low points would end up saying things she would regret like, "I'm going to get in my car and go back to America, bye."

And you know what? There's not one parent on the planet who hasn't said something that they have regretted to their kids in one of those moments where the pressure feels intolerable. So, if you're reading this and fully resonating and feeling it, you're not alone and you're not a bad parent!

Shelby was in Flight!

When you are in a Flight response, you feel:

- Anxious, panicked, and scared.
- Hyperactive, restless, and fidgeting.
- Like escaping and running away.
- Like you will do anything to avoid issues.

When your Habitual Baseline is stuck in the Hustler, you *more often than not*:

- Feel panicky or anxious and look for ways out of the present moment!
- Are constantly on the go, go, go.
- Get stuck "on" and race from task to task.
- May get overly involved before there is actually an issue, intervening out of stress to get things fixed or the opposite.
- Withdraw into "busy" work to have somewhere to "escape" to.

The Hustler feels a low level of anxiety, regardless of the environment. They are always busy, either busy-minded or busy with projects, in order to avoid the present moment. The sympathetic drive of the flight makes them jump in early to fix things that are not yet a problem.

When integrated, the Hustler finally arrives. Right here and now. They realize there is nothing they need to escape from, and they submerge their entire being in their eternal parasympathetic presence.

When you have integrated the Hustler:

- You can stay with difficult feelings without needing to escape.
- You arrive in the present moment.
- Being busy loses its badge of honor.
- Productivity comes from inspiration, not anxiety.
- You can enjoy downtime without scrolling on your phone.
- Quality time doesn't feel like wasted time.
- You feel perfectly okay just as you are right now.

The Gifts of the Hustler

The Hustler Archetype is committed to the momentum of their spirit. If they get the prompt of inspired action, they do it as soon as possible. They don't need to see the full picture; they trust the next steps. Life is about the journey, not the goal. In their positive expression, Hustlers have the potential to create momentum for themselves and others. They are naturally up-regulating and inspire others to take action.

After breathwork, Shelby realized how much she needed to feel in control and that she wasn't in touch with her body. "Now I'm a lot more in touch with my emotions. I didn't understand what my big emotions were growing up, and my parents, bless them, did the best they could do. But they didn't know how to help me interpret what my body was feeling, and that's why I went into avoiding and numbing and drinking, even drinking coffee, not allowing myself to rest."

Her relationship with her daughter has deepened because she is able to communicate with her how she feels before she snaps or follows the urge to run away. When imperfect moments arise, she is able to repair them, which has been deep-repatterning work for Shelby. "I'm more playful. I'm having more fun. I'm dancing. I'm singing. I've been able to just let go and have fun together with them and not be on a perfect timeline. And this morning, while getting ready, it's like time stood still, because usually I'm rushing to get the oldest to preschool, and we were just joking and playing and singing, and I've felt so much more present with my daughter now."

Once an anchor to this point has been created, it's never too far away. The Hustler recognizes when they are trying to leave a moment in time, and they can choose to stay present even when situations feel uncomfortable. They can wait until the "right" moment to take action and enjoy long, slow moments in time and know how to properly soak up an experience.

The Mantra for the Hustler

I let myself arrive. The present moment nurtures me. I trust the timing of life and enjoy riding the wave of right action, responding only when my intuition calls me.

The Avoider: Freeze Response

When you're in Freeze response, life feels like you're stuck in mud. Everything seems overwhelming, and the simplest decisions feel impossible. You might find yourself spacing out during challenging moments, feeling unable to take action, or watching life happen around you without being able to fully participate.

I am going to put up my hand for this Stress Archetype, because most of my reactions are the Avoider! One huge way this played out was that growing up, I just always had this feeling like "I don't get what I want."

I always wanted brand-name things, but my family couldn't afford expensive things, so I'd always get the Kmart version of everything. I always felt like what I truly wanted was out of reach. But knowing what I know now, this was because I was in a state of constant indecision and feeling like I couldn't ask for what I wanted. The thing was, no one actually knew what I wanted. If my mum asked me, I would say, "I don't know!" The Freeze response is like this. It keeps us stuck. We feel blank, unable to intuit, decide, or accurately feel into a moment and then take action.

When responding like an Avoider you may:

- Notice how your mind goes blank.
- Sigh a lot.
- Say, "I don't know" a lot.
- Pretend to not see what your kids are doing.
- Be indecisive.
- Have difficulty making eye contact.

When your Habitual Baseline is stuck in the Avoider, *you more often than not*:

- Feel unable to do anything about the situation.
- Feel like you don't know what you need or what you need to do.
- Often worry about what-ifs.
- Feel disconnected from your intuition.
- Feel out of touch with your body.
- Feel unable to make decisions.

When you have integrated the Avoider, you can:

- Take clear, decisive action rather than feeling stuck
- Get appropriately angry when boundaries are crossed
- Express your needs and desires with confidence
- Feel interested rather than bored
- Stay present in challenging moments without going blank
- Connect with your body's wisdom to guide your decisions

The Gift of the Avoider

The Avoider carries deep wisdom about pause and stillness. They developed this response as a way to stay safe through becoming invisible or "small" when they felt threatened. When integrated, this energy becomes a powerful capacity for contemplation, deep listening, and intuitive knowing. The gift of the Avoider is the ability to be still and observe—it's about learning to use this stillness consciously rather than falling into it reactively.

During my rebirthing breathwork training, in one of my explorations of myself, I discovered a memory of when I was born and being bottle-fed. I re-experienced the deep somatic emotion of the moment that I first experienced a circumstance where "I don't get what I want," which was actually to breast-feed and be connected to my mom. I was taken away from her shortly after birth, and instead of her breast, I was given a bottle. At that moment, I froze. My breath got me in contact with the feeling, and once I unlocked that and saw where I was coming from this whole time (which tracked all the way back to my birth), life really changed! Experiences that once felt unattainable now are my reality, and I was able to trust myself and that I knew the next step and that I could get what I want. This helped me to then know what I want and be free to take steps to creating it!

The Mantra for the Avoider

I am energy in motion. I am connected to this moment through my body, and I savor this moment with all my senses. I flow with life and trust myself to do things that create momentum.

The Pleaser: Fawn Response

Santhiya felt like she had the perfect life. She followed all the rules so that her life went exactly how it had been mapped out.

She was also the first daughter of three girls and felt pressure to get good grades. Her mapped-out life looked like 12 years of education in a mainstream system, then going to university and finding a man, getting engaged, getting married (and you don't move out until you get married), finding a house, building a house, and then having kids.

She followed all of this to a T.

While doing it, she didn't feel suppressed; it was just what people did. And so she didn't feel like she had much choice around it. As long as she was living a life that made her parents and community happy, it seemed like the right thing to do. But in hindsight, she can see how much of her identity and her self-expression were actually being suppressed. She was stuck in pleasing others, which is the Fawn response.

The Fawn response feels like:

- Perfectionism, wanting to get it right.
- People-pleasing.
- Worrying about everyone else.
- Downplaying yourself.
- Not knowing your preferences when someone else is around.

When your Habitual Baseline is stuck in the Pleaser, you *more often than not*:

- Feel like everything is your fault or that you bother people.
- Take too much responsibility to fix situations.
- Apologize a lot unnecessarily.
- Avoid conflict with your kids by keeping them happy or distracting them rather than enforcing boundaries.

- Be overly harsh with your kids to keep others happy in social situations.
- Get caught up in a distorted reality where you are responsible for everyone else's happiness. You are stuck in a cycle of self-abandonment, unable to hear what you need in the noise of people's energy. The constant conforming can be exhausting.

For the Pleaser, they'll experience relief when they shift from overly orienting outward. This brings them home and connects them back to themselves, allowing them to get in touch with themselves, and they can discern where their responsibility begins and ends.

When you have integrated the Pleaser, you can:

- Know your preferences.
- Have a deep commitment to self.
- Trust your body's yes and no.
- Avoid feeling the need to give reasons to justify your preferences.
- Unapologetically express your joy.
- Create win-wins with others.

The Gifts of the Pleaser

The Pleaser Archetype is soft but oh, so strong. They have a gently nonnegotiable self-commitment that heals them from self-betrayal every time they choose themselves. The Pleaser has learned that if they lose, everyone loses. They know that if they commit to creating a win for themselves, they can trust others to create wins for themselves, and the whole process brings everyone closer together. The Pleaser inspires others to become closer to their authentic selves too.

When Santhyia found breathwork, everything started to change and no longer went exactly to plan, but in a good way.

"The things I wanted to do and I imagined for my life but never even would have considered it possible . . . to move away from my family. I could never do that. Or put my kids in a non-mainstream school. I would never do that. Leaving my mainstream medical world job. I just thought that I would do my physio degree, specialize, and work in pediatrics, and that would just be what I did until I retired. But ten years after that, things have really changed. I've taken a different turn. So many changes that I just didn't conceive possible for me. I just have so much trust, so much trust in myself, in the process of life."

Integrating her Fawn stress response brought her more connection with her husband, her kids, and herself. And tangible changes in her life that she couldn't believe. From this place, she no longer felt responsible for the feelings of others, and she could tolerate displeasure from others, staying committed to herself regardless of their feelings.

The Mantra for the Pleaser

I call my energy home to my body. I commit to Self, and I allow others to see me. If I cannot say no, I cannot truly say yes, and so I align cleanly with both. I relish in this true connection with others.

Which Stress Archetype are you?

Take a moment and ask yourself, which of these do you recognize most?

Ask yourself:

- What is your most common Stress Archetype?
- How often are you in this state? Rarely, Sometimes, or More Often than Not?
- If it's only every now and then, what is the specific situation that triggers this reaction for you?
- If it is more often than not, it could be that you are living in survival mode. Do you find that one of the Stress Archetypes is activated even when you are at rest?

For now, all you need to do is reflect and notice which one you are the most often.

Some of you might have found that you are a few different archetypes, or maybe even all. This is totally normal, because we all do have all of these responses; however, most people will have one or two dominant ones. If you can see yourself in all the responses, see if you can distinguish any of the specific triggers that put you into a specific archetype.

For example, maybe you are the Yeller if your kids are fighting, but the Avoider when you have a few hours of free time to hang with the kids. Or maybe your partner brings out the Pleaser in you, and as soon as they leave for work, you are the Yeller with everyone else. See what you can discover about what triggers each Archetype. We will be showing you some simple ways to integrate these responses later in the book, but for now, we just want you to notice.

Now, you might be wondering what the fifth archetype is! And you might have already noticed what is missing! If you are guessing it's the ventral vagal state, you would be correct!

You might remember that we spoke about ventral vagal being the optimal state that we all crave to spend most of our time in. Let's reflect on what it is like to be in ventral vagal.

First of all, you may have heard the saying that life is about the journey, not the destination. Well, you can experience this perspective only if you are in ventral vagal. Ventral vagal allows us to be in the present moment. It arises when we experience signs of safety that give us the message that we can truly put our guard down and enjoy the moment. These might be internal or external messages.

And the paradox is, when you are in this state, even though it's the journey and not the destination, ventral vagal feels like an arrival. It is coming home.

Arrival moments are when stress no longer runs the show and is replaced with more moments of having true compassion for yourself. Or watching the triggers lessen and finding yourself responding to life in whole new ways. And then finding yourself feeling like life wasn't difficult, and instead seeing challenge as an area that simply needed more awareness and compassion. There is an arrival of sorts in that new perspective.

And while of course this doesn't mean there is no stress or that life doesn't become difficult at times, there is in some ways a sense of fulfilment in being able to rely on yourself, regardless of what arises in life.

Maybe you've had a feeling like this before? If so, you were in the fifth archetype, the Reconnected Parent.

If you are in the Reconnected Archetype, when stressed, you:

- Notice, get curious, stay with the sensations and feelings as they arise.
- Have Current States where you experience Hustler, Yeller, Avoider, and Pleaser with growing awareness and return to feeling grounded more quickly each time.

- Approach yourself with kindness despite the stress.
- Feel safe to feel all your feelings, not just the positive ones.
- Have the energy for other people who are dysregulated and can hold space for your loved ones to return to connection.
- Increasingly live from a place of authenticity and have space to dream big, create, and thrive. You feel lit up about what you have to contribute to the world.
- Are able to prioritize activities that help you stay connected to yourself, knowing it serves others. You can be with your kid's dysregulation and stay authentically grounded and intuit what is needed.
- Have increasingly authentic relationships.
- Feel satisfied at the end of each day.

The Mantra for the Reconnected Parent

All parts of me arrive in the present moment. I am the safe, strong space my inner child and my kids need, a creator and tender of visions and dreams. I am.

If you have never experienced this before, or if you want more moments like these (who doesn't?), then let's look at how to use the Stress Archetypes to discover what is stored in your autonomic signature and how to integrate it so your baseline is more aligned with the Reconnected Parent.

This is what the next two chapters are all about!

CHAPTER 8

Embracing the Gifts of Parenting—Emma

Pain travels in families until someone is willing to feel it.
— STEPHI WAGNER

Quite a few years ago, we had a photographer work on a version of the Reconnected Parenting course, and after they had done all the visuals for the content and were wrapping up the project, they said, "I am not sure about having kids anymore!" They didn't have any kids yet, and after reading about triggers and designing the audio covers for the practices on how to let go of parental guilt and more, they were confronted by their doubts of whether they wanted to have kids at all!

And fair enough! All of this talk about how triggering parenting is, how we get forced into upleveling beyond our own childhood patterns, how dysregulated we can get, and how we can't avoid personal work in order to be the parent we want to be, you would be forgiven for finding it off-putting or daunting! You might remember back in Chapter 1, when Eleanor recognized that her suppressed anger patterns had been passed on to her kids! The first thing she said was, "No one told me about this, and I already have kids!"

Knowing that we might pass on patterns can be so daunting.

We've noticed that sometimes people decide they will do all the personal work they need to do before they have kids, assuming that this will mean that they are immune from passing down patterns and suppressed stress to their children.

Unfortunately, it doesn't work like that!

However, we have a different perspective for you to try. What if parenting was actually the most opportune circumstance possible for healing, self-awareness, transformation, and growth? What if parenting shows you more about yourself than you will learn on any retreat, no matter how much you meditate, how many ceremonies you attend, how many self-help books you read, or how much therapy you do?

We believe that parenting is the fastest, quickest way to get directly in touch with what is really happening in our nervous system (there is no hiding!), and at the same time it is the urgent motivation we need to go where we need to go to integrate the stored stressors affecting our baseline! It's better than any retreat, therapy, therapist, plant medicine, meditation, and is the catalyst many of us need to grow!

Relate? Let's take it a step further.

Something else starts to happen once we step into doing the work of integrating the stress in our nervous system, acknowledging our emotions, and dealing with our triggers. We've touched on what happens when someone starts to step into ventral vagal more often—they are rewiring their Habitual Baseline to a Reconnected Baseline. As we deal with the things we don't want to pass on to our kids, do you know what happens? We get more and more in touch with our true and authentic self and step into the Reconnected Parent Archetype. And even better, we become more able to express that part of us.

A Reconnected community member said the coolest thing to us recently after learning about their Stress Archetype:

"I just realized that my Stress Archetype is not who I really am! I thought I was a cranky, impatient person. I am not. That is just

my stress response! I have created an entire sense of self and identity around what I am like when I am stressed! Who I am underneath, this is something I am very ready to discover!" —Reconnected community share

If we are open to the gifts of personal growth our kids bring to us, we can completely transform our relationship to ourselves, to other people, and to life itself. If we are willing to consciously be aware of our triggers, then parenting stress can be something that helps us grow in self-awareness, heal our own childhood "stuff," and step into being the person we want to be! Parenting can be the catalyst for self-actualization!

For this reason, at The Reconnected we say, "The children are the gurus."

We often think about adults passing wisdom on to children, and of course, there is truth in that—we guide them, they need us—but it's not the whole picture. We can be living our lives absolutely comfortably, without much of a call to reflect or aspire to change the way we relate to ourselves and to life. And then we have children, and they catalyze a process of healing the parts of our nervous system that are reactive and stuck in the past. In many ways, self-work is initiated in us by our children, and in this sense, they are the greatest teachers we have! All they need from us is for us to say yes to the invitation!

Maybe you've heard Eleanor tell the story of living down the road from an Indigenous Elder, who would take a daily walk past her house each morning at the exact time that she was trying to wrangle four kids under five years old into the car to get the eldest to kindergarten. She would pop her head in and kiss the babies, hug the toddlers, and say to Eleanor, "So beautiful, and all you need to do is receive their love and return it." If you have heard the story being told, it is with a lot of humor about how far from that state of mind Eleanor was in the moment, rushing around in Hustler mode!

In many families, we pass down dysfunctional patterns and Stress Archetypes and repeat them from generation to generation. Think back to the story of my dad's war trauma, and how aspects of this trauma were still affecting the way I related to my kids decades later!

My dad was a highly sensitive being who experienced horrific traumas at war. When my dad returned from the war, he was suspicious of authority, he drank a lot, and while he was incredibly sweet-hearted, he was absolutely an Avoider. He was traumatized from the war and had many things that would trigger him to shut down his feelings.

As well as being in a war as a young man, my dad had also grown up on a farm in Australia in the '50s, on a low income. And he had a very ingrained sense of "suck it up" mentality. His favorite thing to say when I complained was "suck a stone" in jest. So, as well as being constantly told not to cry, I couldn't recall seeing my parents cry during my life. I think I've seen my mother cry once! My dad, never. However, had you asked me before I had the aha moment about how suppressed my emotions were, I would have said my childhood was a complete happy one! Despite my dad being traumatized in a lot of ways, and unable to be with my emotions, he was playful, he was fun, and we had so many memories of going swimming and connecting outdoors.

However, on an emotional level, I was not given what I needed. While it was not a highly traumatic experience, I didn't have someone who was able to be attuned to or sensitive to my emotions. I never had a mature, safe, adult nervous system with me when I had big feelings. I can now recognize that this was a "little *t* trauma" that I carried into adulthood.

This meant there were a lot of things that triggered me when I was an adult! And especially when I became a parent. Because my dad couldn't be there for me, it became impossible for me to be there for my own kids in certain areas. Any kind of big, loud emotions made me feel tense and slightly frozen. Like my dad, I was definitely the Avoider Archetype. Whenever there were big, loud emotions, even if it was joy, and especially if it was some kind of "scream and run around" type game, I was out! I got immediately tense and distracted, waiting for an accident or something bad to happen. I would vacate mentally and emotionally by putting on some headphones or physically leaving the room.

If the kids played like that all day, my reaction was to put everyone in the car and go for a drive or get outside so I could have space from it all. It was my way of escaping. While it was not necessarily a negative pattern, it was not completely coming from a place where I was free to choose my response. It was an expression of the emotional suppression that my dad used to survive being in a war.

The pattern that was passed down is that loud, big emotions are triggers for my nervous system, and the Avoider is my Stress Archetype in those moments.

You might have heard the saying "We repeat what we don't repair." Often that saying is interpreted as "We pass down patterns to our kids that we don't repair for ourselves," but another way of looking at it is this:

Any limiting experiences or beliefs that do not align with your authentic self will be unconsciously re-created by our psyche-body-mind, again and again until we are ready to confront and integrate the stress that is underneath. In fact, the areas where we feel the most stuck in a pattern or way of relating that feel familiar and that we are fed up with are actually the very areas that our nervous system is most ready to resolve and integrate.

Dr. Lisa Dion is a play therapist who calls the way kids project their past onto the present so that they can resolve it the "setup." Renowned psychotherapist Allan Schore calls this an *enactment*—whereby we are ready to replay something from the past, in a safe place, so we can resolve it. Yet I think we can all relate to the way that we have the same thing happen over and over until we get so fed up, we are ready to change! This is also a setup! It's just one that we don't normally notice. And, let's face it, parenting and our closest relationships are the main areas where we see repeating patterns. These often reflect our implicit sense of self. But what if, rather than despairing about being stuck in ways of relating we aren't happy with, we instead see the repeating pattern as a sign that we are getting ready to clear it and are close to doing things differently?

When I started to do breathwork, I was given a huge opportunity to integrate a lot of the stress that I had experienced as a child whose emotions were too big for everyone around me. I released the layers of suppression around crying and became freer and freer to just feel my own feelings. In fact, my feelings became guides for me that I tend to frequently!

One thing that happened was, I went from feeling that loud noises from my kids were intolerable to having more and more space for their feelings. And with five kids, including twin toddlers, my house is in a constant state of noise, and now I even jump in and initiate loud, fun games! Parenting from a Reconnected Baseline rather than my Habitual Baseline is so freeing!

What did we need?

It can be simple to think that we needed our parents to do things differently. In some cases, this is true. However, in most circumstances, all we really needed was to be seen, heard, and acknowledged by someone who was attuned to our experience and who could feel okay with what we were expressing.

Once we are an adult, we can actually give this to ourselves. But it isn't our conscious mind that needs this. It is our subconscious and our somatic-emotional self that needs tending to, which needs to happen in our nervous system, and the best way to do this is through the breath. Here is an example of how this part of us comes up in breathwork sessions to be integrated.

Chrissy came to breathwork feeling like she had a lot to work to do personally after a traumatic childhood. During her first sessions, she was so distressed by other people crying, she felt like it was her job to make everyone stop crying or something bad might happen. She had grown up in an abusive household, where everyone was punished if one person cried. She was stuck in fawning because she had learned that she had to keep others happy to be safe. One session, she had a profound experience of having a facilitator sit next to her while she was feeling sad about how her childhood was. This was a totally new experience for her. And she had a huge epiphany. She said: "I did not realize my whole life no one ever stayed with me while I felt something. And so I've never been able to stay with my daughter now too. And I can give it to her now. I cannot unsee or unknow this now! I had no reference for understanding this was what I needed. But I have got it now. I know what a safe presence feels like now. I know what she needs."

Her trigger was other people's tears; the Stress Archetypes activated were the Pleaser and the Avoider. With the root cause of this trigger integrated, she could go toward her daughter's crying, realizing what she needed and being able to give her what she had never had herself, now that her body had a reference for it!

When this rewire happens in your nervous system, it is profound. Inspiring, huh? Want to apply it to your own life?

Let's start to take some embodied action in the next chapter on the breath!

But first, to get out of the automatic and habitual and start to become intentional and conscious, we will begin with a journaling activity to prepare you for the next chapter, where we will show you how the breath can be used to rewire.

Time to put this into practice...

What triggered me today? Which Stress Archetype was activated?

Is this a familiar or repeating pattern in my life or in my relationships? Where else does it play out?

How did I respond?

How would I prefer this area of my life to be? If I could choose how it went, how would I be able to respond?

See if you can identify:

- The Trigger
- The Overreaction
- The Stress Archetype

Asking yourself how you would prefer it to be is the first step to making automatic, unconscious reactions hardwired in your nervous system and bringing them into your conscious life! For now, let go of needing to know how you will get there and just allow yourself to express how you would rather be able to respond in those moments. This is your intention!

Take this intention with you to the next chapter, where we are going to simply show you how you can begin to take this new way of relating into your nervous system.

CHAPTER 9

Breath and the Nervous System—Eleanor

When you activate your gut feelings and listen to your heartbreak—when you follow the interoceptive pathways to your innermost recesses—things begin to change.

— BESSEL VAN DER KOLK

"As I was breathing, I felt rage passing through my body and got complete clarity about the sense of conflict I have when being my authentic self.

"This energy from my childhood was about being blamed for a mess I didn't make, then being punished when I became angry at my sister for lying while I tried to tell my truth. It was a shocking experience of feeling emotionally abandoned, disempowered, and enraged about being falsely accused. From that day on, any disagreement or difference of opinion from my mother always felt more threatening than it was. I adapted by picking up cues and adjusting my responses.

"Ultimately, at the time, I was punished for expressing anger more than anything else.

"A clear and direct message came through today while I was breathing: 'Love the me that is full of rage.' It felt absolutely liberating.

"Interestingly, I have explored that incident in therapy but have never had the full-body experience." —Luana, Reconnected community member

When we consciously return our breath to an optimal breathing pattern and stay with whatever arises, anything that has been kept trapped in the body-mind comes up in our awareness so that we can release it from our body.

What is the value of this?

As we were writing this book, we reached out to Luana to ask her what had integrated in her life after the experience she had had in her session. After all, we are less interested in having experiences in breathwork sessions and more interested in seeing our lives change and go in the direction of our intentions!

Five months after that experience, Luana had this to say:

"That breathwork session was pivotal in order for me to reclaim a lost part of myself. It's so clear to see how accumulated traumas led me into freeze/fawn and the Pleaser mode as a survival mechanism.

"Before that breathwork session, the Pleaser was my Habitual Baseline!

"Since then, I've noticed that I am much less willing to automatically slip into Pleaser mode. This is big for me! I'm guilt-free when claiming healthy boundaries. In the past, I might state a boundary accompanied by an explanation or excuse. No more!

"I have also had more awareness in some really powerful moments when I have started to abandon myself again. Recently I found myself trying to figure out what someone else might want to hear instead of saying what was true for me. Caught myself and thought to myself, 'Stop, why am I doing this?' And I just changed it instantly!" —Luana, Reconnected Community member

Far from just being something that we can use to calm ourselves down when we are angry or upset (i.e., using your breath as a Band-Aid!), the breath can be used to gently and safely integrate stressful and limiting experiences: "little *t* traumas" (like the one in the story above), "big *T* traumas" (with support), limiting beliefs, and any type of experience that drives the reactivity and dysregulation, keeping us stuck in loops of relating to life, ourselves, and other people in ways that just don't serve us anymore.

You might remember from earlier in the book that I spent my research year looking at the way that gentle, subtle breathwork influenced people's at-rest Nervous-System Baseline. I discovered that our inhale and exhale directly stimulate the vagus nerve (for a recap, revisit Chapter 5), which also has a relationship to the limbic system that stores our childhood memories and emotions. The mechanisms that are likely behind the way that stored experiences can be released and integrated via the breath were starting to be clear!

One way to live in greater and greater states of ventral vagal when we are at rest (our Reconnected Baseline) is to integrate the past experiences that create the high levels of stress in our Habitual Baseline. This chapter is going to outline the link between the breath and the nervous system, but we will be going way deeper than using the breath to calm ourselves and show how, in fact, in some circumstances, when we try to stay calm, we can accidentally use our breath to add more stress to our nervous system!

How are the breath and nervous system linked?

Have you ever been stressed or upset about something, and someone has told you to take a deep breath? It is a common phrase used when it is time to pause because things are getting heated! It is in our collective understanding that if you're angry or upset, you just need to stop and breathe, and you will calm down enough to deal rationally with whatever situation is upsetting you. Without realizing it, this phrase is based on the neurobiology of breathing! See, the ANS and therefore our survival and safety mechanisms, are completely linked with our breathing mechanism!

For example, have you noticed that when you get a shock or a fright, you gasp for air? Or maybe you have noticed that when you are distracted or feeling low, you might hold your breath or breathe shallowly a lot of the time. Have you ever noticed that when you go out into nature and feel relaxed, you naturally take a deep breath? Or that when you cuddle up with your kids and feel how much you love them, you naturally soak in the moment by savoring a slow and full breath? The complex, multilayered relationship between wellness, breathing, our nervous system, and how we relate to the world is so fascinating! Another very interesting thing in the research is that shallow, inhibited, or any type of non-optimal disordered breathing is also related to high levels of stress when at rest!

Your Breath and Your Nervous System

Our lungs are directly linked to our ANS through the vagus nerve. The vagus nerve is one of 12 cranial nerves, which are the nerves at the back of the brain that control your senses and some aspects of movement, like facial expressions. You will remember from Chapter 5 that the vagus nerve is the brake on hyperarousal. The ventral vagus (the front of the vagus nerve) is active when we are in an ideal state of arousal, and the dorsal vagus (the back of the vagus nerve) is active when we go into parasympathetic overload, or hypoarousal. (The vagus nerve is called the wandering nerve because it is the longest nerve in our body, wandering from the medulla oblongata in the brain stem and traveling down through the neck and thorax, passing behind the root of the lung, and extending into the abdomen.)

The Vagal Nerve & Pulmonary Plexus

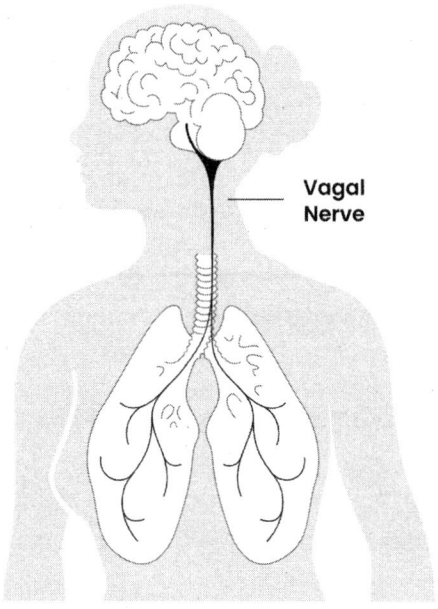

As the vagus nerve descends into the thorax, it extends several branches to the lungs, known as the pulmonary branches. These branches form the pulmonary plexus, a network of nerves that link to the bronchial tubes, bronchioles, and lung tissue. It is the vagus nerve that links breathing with the homeostasis of not only our physical body but also our emotions, our thoughts, our spirituality, and our relationships.

The relationship between the breath and these parts of our experience is bi-directional. For example, when we feel an emotion, our breathing sometimes changes in response to the feeling, and we can also change the way we feel emotionally by adjusting our breathing. The relationship between the breath and emotion goes both ways; they influence each other. For example, when we cry or are upset, we naturally breathe faster in and out through the mouth, and there is likely a corresponding sympathetic activation in our nervous system. Then, say we hear someone coming and we don't want them to know we are upset, we instinctively breathe in through the nose and slow down our breath to control our emotions; we will feel a little calmer, and the feelings will subside a little—our parasympathetic hand brake is on!

Or perhaps we are lucky enough that the person who is approaching is a safe person, and when they arrive, we cry harder for a moment with them, and once the feeling is totally expressed and we authentically feel better, our breath naturally lengthens and slows down, we might sigh out in relief, and we feel grounded again, landing in that Reconnected Parent Archetype in a ventral vagal state. Such an incredible, complex interplay between emotions, thought, relationship, self-connection, relationship to life and spirituality, and our breathing all interlinked in a large part thanks to the vagus nerve.

Incredible, huh?

Let's also reflect on how our breath, being a part of the ANS, is most of the time automatic, unconscious, and habitual. Isn't it so fortunate and well-designed that we don't need to think about consciously breathing each breath! Yet, miraculously, out of our autonomic functions, breathing is the one automatic function we can easily make conscious. We cannot consciously change our heartbeat any more than we can stop sweating if we get too hot! However, we can at any moment become aware of our breathing and control it.

When we master our breathing, we can master aspects of the other functions that the vagus nerve links to that otherwise can feel out of our control, like thinking and emotions. This is why people associate calm breathing with regulating emotions. And it's true! We often think about the breath as being a way to calm our emotions, but this is a reflection of a couple of things. One is that, broadly speaking, most people still feel that all their problems would be solved if they could just stay calm more often. A lot of the research on the vagus nerve and breathing focuses on how our breathing influences the functioning of the nervous system. The before-and-after studies demonstrate that we can change our Current State in the moment with our breathing rather than trying to improve our Habitual Baseline levels.

And you will know by now that that is what we are all about!

While, obviously, if you can go from feeling ragey to less ragey before you lose it at your kids by taking a deep breath, you should by all means take a breath, but it is profound to acknowledge that that is a Band-Aid and also such a small fraction of what is possible with conscious breathing.

What we are pioneering here is an understanding that the breath can be used to integrate past stressors so that we no longer experience the triggers, and so we won't need to calm ourselves down! Because we are already operating from a ventral vagal space! How to use your conscious breathing to create a Reconnected Baseline of ventral vagal—so you can spend less time in your life being the Yeller, the Avoider, the Hustler, or the Pleaser and instead be the Reconnected Archetype more often—is what we are teaching about here.

Reconnected Breathing for Nervous-System Integration: Becoming Safe to Feel and Expanding Your Baseline and Flexibility

To optimize your breathing for activating the parasympathetic nervous system, breathe in and out through your nose, gently using the entire breathing mechanism, including the belly, the lower chest, and the upper chest. Your breath should slow right down with minimal effort.

Optimal Breathing

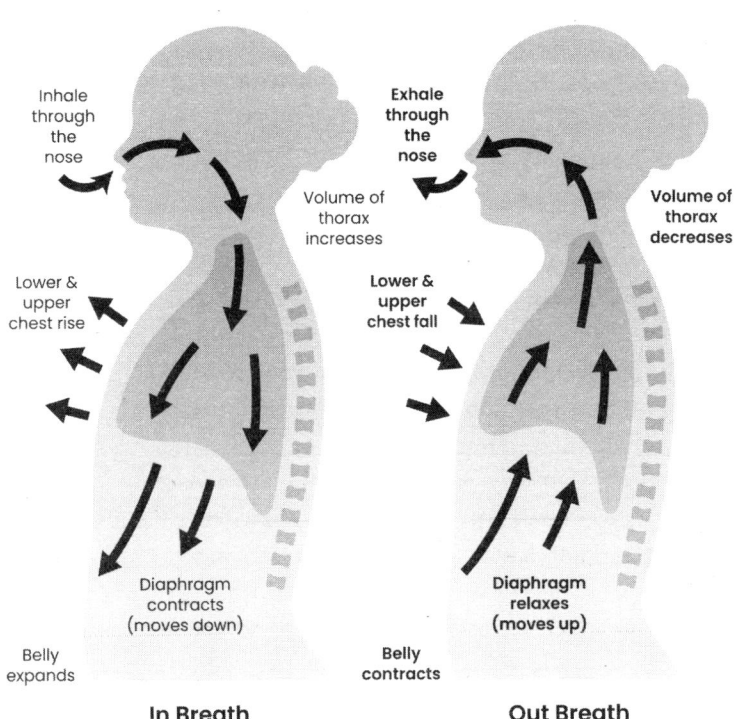

Rather than using this type of breathing to calm emotions (which, by the way, have you noticed can actually be pushing feelings away?), you can use the same breath to do three important things that lead over time to integration of stored stress:

1. Give your body the message "I am safe to feel" through a parasympathetic-activating breath.

2. Create a safe internal space for you to move toward and stay with feelings and emotions that you would normally suppress and avoid, including emotions like joy, peace, and happiness, which are just as often suppressed as emotions like anger and fear.
3. Give your nervous system the message on a somatic-emotional level, "I see you, I hear you, I care, and I understand."

What happens when we breathe in this way?
We widen our capacity to feel.

While you are breathing, you will have either a Release of dysregulation or a new Anchor to ventral vagal or a mix of both. Releasing experiences happen when we feel safe enough to be with states of mild dysregulation—physically, mentally, emotionally, and spiritually. This might feel like sensations of restlessness, discomfort, tension, or emotions (such as anger, sadness, frustration, apathy, and boredom), thoughts and images, or awareness of memories or experiences. With the breath staying completely relaxed and subtle, with no force or pressure, we set an ideal container for ourselves to regulate and integrate past experiences. Our body knows how to go step-by-step and with safety.

Yep, this is not breathing to relax or to be calm, although those states can and do arise spontaneously! Anchoring experiences are moments when our nervous system is in a Ventral Vagal state. Anchoring experiences can be a feeling of pleasure, a sense of being affirmed, knowing you are safe and held by the world, a sense of peace, calmness, positive thoughts or imagery, inspirational thoughts, or any other experience that you feel nourished by. You might even drift off to sleep, which can be incredibly restorative.

But we are not counting the breath, trying to make the inhale longer than the exhale. Nor are we observing our experience with detachment as in meditation.

Breathing to Rewire and "Balance Your Baseline"

So, if we aren't counting our breath, aiming to relax, and we don't "witness" the experience as you might in meditation, then what are we doing? Alakh Analda describes the breathwork process as being a "self-generated, self-mastery" process, that is essentially "the self, revealing itself, to itself."[1] One of the things that I have come to notice over many years of walking in two worlds of mainstream therapy and the once-fringe breathwork world is that so many of the modifications in this parasympathetic branch of breathwork are ahead of the game in terms of giving people the power to do deep rewiring safely and easily, while also putting people into, as Emma says, "the driver's seat of their life" thanks to highly practical ways of embodying intentional, conscious living principles.

Using the breath as described above, in and out through the nose, fuller than your habitual breathing, allowing the breath to be relaxed with no pressure or force, we set in motion the unwinding of our nervous system with the support of a key attitude.

"Stay with everything that arises."

So many practices mirror the survival mechanisms that inhibit or deny our experience, attempting to cultivate calm by overriding and inhibiting our body sensations, thoughts, and emotions. What if, instead, we moved toward any and all experiences with curiosity? What happens when we *stay with* all facets of our experience: physical, emotional, mental, and spiritual?

What countless hours of breathwork have shown is that when we activate the parasympathetic nervous system with a gentle breath, and then adopt an attitude of curiosity and willingness to move toward our experience, our body and breath give us the exact experience we need to unburden our nervous system from stored stress in our Habitual Baseline.

This is the process of integration.

When we stay with the sensations in our body, we can very safely and easily experience body memories and allow a discharge of the stress that those memories still hold for us. This can be like having a body memory recall of times when we stored stress when we were younger, but essentially the experience that we have when we do this practice is completely unique to our personal autonomic signature.

When we bring an attitude of curiosity and make no experience wrong, a deeply personal, unique, authentic unwinding experience can happen for our nervous system. And the experience that happens is sometimes not what we expect!

We can sometimes believe that in order to heal from the past, we need to release or revisit past challenges. This can happen, yet our bodies are so wise that the process of unwinding is always what we are ready for and what we need, and sometimes this is actually a strengthening experience. For example, sometimes what arises for us when we start breathing is happiness and laughter. Or a sense of being in touch with ourselves. Or deep peace or trust in life.

The experiences that happen are spontaneous and authentic; they are not forced (because the breath is not forced!). At the same time, we can cultivate an ideal relationship with ourselves by being more attuned to our own needs. As adults, we can give ourselves what we needed when we were little but may not have received. We can let ourselves be seen, heard, and validated in all aspects of our experience. This gives the inner parts of ourselves exactly what we have always needed, and when we feel it in our bodies, we rewire a sense of having what we needed then.

What happens when we use our breath in this way?

Let's hear from Vanda, a Reconnected community member, for an example of how this might look or unfold:

"*My four-year-old is a little wiggly worm. She always was. One of those kids that needs her batteries drained all the way before falling asleep.*

"*She can't stay still at bedtime when snuggling in bed. This was so triggering for me. I wondered, What the heck is wrong with her? I even snapped at her in frustration once, 'Why are you like this?'*

"*I reacted with excessive rage about this innocent yet annoying thing, so disproportionate to the situation. My amount of anger was so high, I swear I could charge up a rocket to Mars. Through Reconnected Parenting, I did know that it wasn't her, it was me, but that didn't help at all. I was so pissed off at her! In order to try to keep this rage at bay in bed with her, I was doing a daily Reconnected Breathwork audio to connect with myself and track my sensations and emotions. I'd do this all the time to keep myself grounded and away from a rage fit. Yet I was often so pissed off that after bedtime, I often went at my punching bag to release it! Then one night as I lay there at bedtime, doing a breathwork session and lying next to her, I had this memory come up.*

"*I used to be the same!*

"*My brother and I shared a bedroom, and we would party at bedtime: laugh, sing, and generally muck up! My parents would separate us for the evening and put me in their bedroom to fall asleep, and they would physically hold me down, restrain me, until I fell asleep.*

"*With this memory, it dawned on me!*

"When my daughter wiggles, my body remembers this and wants to do the same to my daughter. I want to hold her down! Stop her from moving! I am so triggered by the wiggling! Me letting her wiggle, to do this thing I was not allowed to do, makes my body berserk. The rage I felt was a body memory of a time when I was helpless, and my body wanted to repeat the pattern.

"I was so sorry for little me, and the pull to repeat this was so strong. I totally understood in that moment how abused people abuse others. It's visceral. My heart breaks still at the thought of how we misunderstand ourselves. I am not saying I was abused. My parents did the best they could. They were actually sweet and empowering but handled this bedtime struggle in a way that left a strong mark.

"So grateful to breathwork that it brought me back to realize that my out-of-proportion rage was a body memory. It wasn't me being a monster; it wasn't my daughter being a naughty child. It was just this unprocessed, stuck-in-time experience.

"I am happy to report that while it took some time for me to take the charge out of bedtime, I am so happy to report we got there. I still get annoyed, but it is proportional to what is actually happening."
—Vanda, Reconnected community member

Can you hear a few key things in this share?

- The Trigger: Bedtime
- The Overreaction: Rage
- The Stress Archetype: the Yeller
- The Release, Anchor, and/or Insight: Anger from being restrained as a child at bedtime
- The Integration: "I can be with my child at bedtime."

Can you imagine how this would take her Habitual Baseline an integrated step toward the Reconnected Baseline? Her breath released a body memory stored in her nervous system that was being triggered during bedtime and causing an overreaction. After this release, she became freer to choose how she responded to the wiggling. Read the next share below and see if you can identify Natalie's process as you read—she had an Anchoring experience. See if you can identify:

- The Trigger
- The Overreaction
- The Stress Archetype
- The Release, Anchor, and/or Insight
- The Integration

"When I was growing up, my parents were very preoccupied with their own lives and their own problems, and I knew this, but I had no idea the impact that it had had on me until I started breathwork. A major turning point happened for me when I had a very strengthening experience one day. I was doing some breathwork and started to feel sadness arising. I had a feeling of Emma and Eleanor being there with me on the other side of the camera, guiding the session.

"I suddenly felt an overwhelming sense of being held. It literally felt like someone was carrying me physically and emotionally, and that I was so loved. More loved than I realized.

"I had this sudden urge to roll to one side and go to sleep, and then it hit me: I was giving myself what I had never had. No one had ever stayed with me while I went to sleep, and I was giving myself the feeling of people 'being there' for me while I slept.

"It felt like I was getting a total download in my cells for something that I never knew I was missing.

"In that exact moment, I saw how I had never been able to give my kids this either. I didn't really know they even needed me

at bedtime! I made them do it on their own and got them in trouble if they came out of the room or needed me in any way.

"I knew instantly it was because I couldn't give what I didn't get, but also that I had 'it' now in my body, what presence feels like.

"I am proud to say, since that day, I have given my kids more connection than ever before and can see when they need it! It blows me away that I had no reference point in my body for presence before this moment." —Natalie, Reconnected community member

Isn't that a profound share?

- The Trigger: Being needed at bedtimes
- The Overreaction: Withdrawing
- The Stress Archetype: Avoider
- The Release, Anchor, and/or Insight: Anchored to a feeling of being safe and loved. Insight that she had never received this from her parents, so she couldn't give it to her kids.
- The Integration: "I can give my kids what I never had."

Can you see how the breath helped to access and release the original incident that was stored in the nervous system, but that it was directly related to the number-one area in which each parent was currently experiencing difficulty? And this leads us to another important aspect of this work!

Creative Versus Reactive Living

The area of our life that we are most challenged by, or most inspired to do differently, is the area of our nervous system that is also most ready to unwind any associated stressors.

In the bedtime shared above, you can hear how much pain bedtime is causing for this mumma! And in the second part, the part that you may have missed was that this parent was so desperate to connect with her two kids, but she couldn't figure out why she was avoidant of connection with them!

The areas we are struggling in are actually the areas where we are most ready to grow—and where our nervous system is most ready to transform. Usually, these are the parts of life where we are most reactive. In fact, we are unconscious, automatic, and habitual about them. But what if, instead of being reactive, we could be more consciously creative and intentional?

How can we do this? How do we go from reactivity to creativity? The first step is to be conscious of what our reaction is and the automatic, habitual ways we do not want to behave, think, or feel anymore.

Then, we ask ourselves, "How would I prefer to be?"

Being creative instead of reactive starts by literally thinking about how we would like to feel, think, and respond instead! Creation starts with an idea of what we would like to have happening that is not yet happening. And this preferred future is our intention for our life! Intentions are the first step toward life going in the direction you choose, and they are most powerful when they are about the area of life that we are currently most triggered in. To be intentional we need to:

Identify the most active trigger for you at the moment.

Identify the reaction/overreaction.

Identify the Stress Archetype you are in at that time.

And then, take some time to journal *how you would prefer this area to be*! Let's do that right now. Take some time to journal about how you would prefer to be able to respond and how you would feel about yourself and your kids when you are able to do this!

For example:

- The Trigger: Bedtimes
- The Overreaction: Rage when my daughter wiggles
- The Stress Archetype: the Yeller
- The Intention: To be able to help my daughter fall asleep peacefully feeling loved and to feel peaceful myself during bedtimes

Expressing an intention is the first step out of automatic, reactive, survival-brain ways of relating and stepping into more mindful, self-aware, and ventral vagal states for yourself.

An intention is always a future-focused, positive description of how you prefer life to be.

Once you are clear on your intention, the second step is to breathe consciously, activating the parasympathetic nervous system, and stay with whatever arises, allowing your nervous system to give you either a releasing experience or an anchoring experience.

Over time, this process reduces the stress load on your nervous system, massively expands your window of tolerance and capacity to be safe to feel, and gives you new ways to relate to yourself, life, and other people.

Important: Even though the practice seems simple, for some nervous systems even breathing a fuller-than-usual breath can be activating. Remember you can let go of the practice at any time, and if you have any medical conditions or mental health concerns, please consult your healthcare provider before participating. We recommend you keep your personal Breathwork practice to 15 minutes unless you have the support of a qualified facilitator.

Guided Practice

Let's take a break from learning about the why behind the breath and have an experience of what we are talking about!
Create five minutes of undisturbed space.
Start by journaling.

- The Trigger: What area of your life do you find the most challenging at the moment?
- The Reaction or Overreaction: When you're triggered, what happens? How do you think, feel, behave?
- The Stress Archetype: Which of the Stress Archetypes are being activated?
- The Intention: How would you prefer to feel when the trigger happens? How would you prefer to respond? Feel? Think? Go deep into the details of what you would rather have happening in that moment. Now ask yourself, if I could create that, what would it give me? Find an overall word, like peace or pride, that you would experience if you were able to transform this trigger and reaction.

When you have written all of that down, repeat it aloud and see what happens in your body! Speaking aloud an intention that really means something to you usually has a tangible response in your body. Keep adding to your intention till it really makes you smile, if you can!

Now, lie down or sit down, and you will spend five minutes tuning in to this nervous system through your breath.

You do not need to focus on the intention or the trigger for this activity. In fact, you will completely let go of thinking about it.

From this moment, you will stay with everything that spontaneously and authentically arises while you are breathing.

Bring your awareness to your breathing without changing anything. Notice the quality of your breathing: Is it shallow, deep, fast or slow, through the nose or mouth? Just notice.

Then, start breathing in and out through the nose and make your breath slower and fuller than usual.

While you do this, stay with everything that arises: body sensations, feelings, thoughts, memories, visuals, and any type of spiritual experience that might arise.

If you feel like crying, just cry. If you feel like laughing, just laugh. You can also move, stretch, wriggle your fingers and toes, and follow any prompts your body might give you.

We recommend you do this for just five minutes to begin with when you are practicing at home for self-development. Because of the wisdom of your psyche, you will have only an experience that you are safe to feel.

Set a timer, or perhaps play a five-minute song to keep the time.

After this, you can journal the following:

How does what you experience while you were breathing relate to your triggers, your overreaction, or your intention?

Ask yourself, was the experience:

Releasing: any experience that is like an amplification of the trigger or overreaction or your Stress Archetype, i.e., if your overreaction is frustration, and you are stuck being the Yeller, a releasing session would be feeling the frustration for you to stay with and release.

Insightful: any experience that brings insight or awareness about why you do what you do, like a memory recall of where the trigger came from, or something that puts you in touch with the original wound along with an opportunity to see, hear, and understand yourself at a deeper level.

Anchoring: any experience that is the embodiment of your intentions, like peace, joy, or strength. And any experience that is new or that strengthens you in some way. Anchoring experiences connect you with positive things you want more of in life. Sometimes it might be the first time you have ever had this feeling. Many people say, "I felt safe in my body for the first time." Anchoring leaves us feeling more resourced in life.

You can use this practice when you are triggered or save it for when you have time, or even while you are dropping off to sleep.

If you would like to follow a practice video, go to: www.thereconnected.com/book

Integration

When we completely integrate an issue, it resolves to the point that we can't remember having an issue, we no longer are triggered around that issue, and we are free to choose our responses in similar circumstances. Sometimes we take a quantum leap in integration, but most commonly we go step-by-step as we are ready.

Reflecting on what we integrated as we were breathing is helpful, but sometimes we don't have any clear sign of what we integrated until we go back out into life, see how our responses and reactions have changed, and experience where our baseline is at after our breathwork session.

Reconnected Baseline Becomes Your Habitual Baseline

Over time, after integrating the stored stress that impacts your Habitual Baseline, you will find yourself living from a more Reconnected Baseline.

Moving Toward a Reconnected Baseline

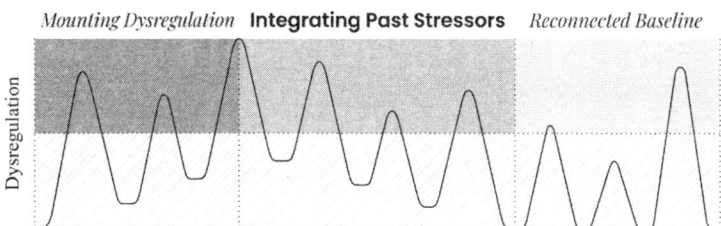

Trusting the Process

A paradigm shift comes when you have applied this process enough times that the next time you see a pattern repeating or feel a familiar emotion or trigger, instead of feeling swept up in it, you feel excited about having something to breathe on!

You know that if you have challenges in life, or if a reenactment of a past hurt is coming up, this means that this pattern is ready to transform or release. You will know how to set an intention and that it is time to use your breath to allow your nervous system to unwind.

In this moment, you have arrived in a well-earned trust in the process.

What now?

Incorporating this practice and these attitudes will move you step-by-step toward being the Reconnected Parent Archetype.

Most parents, once they learn this information, are really interested in how to raise kids so that they do not have to store so much stress in their nervous systems and they can grow up with self-awareness and a Reconnected Baseline from the start! The next chapter is all about this! Let's learn more about your child's nervous system before diving into the Whole Family Nervous System in Section III.

SECTION II

understanding your child's nervous system

CHAPTER 10

Your Child's Nervous System—Eleanor

I am here—I hear you—I understand—I care—I delight in you!
— GARRY LANDRETH

Before we start this chapter, it is a good time to pause and take a breath.

Inhale.

Exhale.

Many parents, once they become aware of how the nervous system works and the way it holds our entire life experience, can get very stressed about their children's nervous systems!

And rightly so! It is profound to realize how much our life experiences impact us and to take paradigm-shifting perspectives that help us to really understand what is happening for ourselves and our children.

Nothing is more important than our kids' well-being.

However, one thing we have seen time and time again is parents who come to this work and want to jump quickly to "fixing" their kids, or feel highly anxious or worried about preventing hard things happening to their kids, or feel bad about having yelled at their kids in the past and like it's too late to raise them the way they want to.

Three important things to keep in mind:

1. It's never too late.
2. You are here, doing the work.
3. The first step is taking care of *your* nervous system.

An important gentle reminder before we start this chapter: your children's well-being is largely determined by what is held in your nervous system. Your nervous system is their safe space and where many of the impressions that form their personal autonomic signature come from! So please don't skip doing the breathwork from Chapter 9, and never underestimate the power of creating your own self-connection and increasing your own Ventral Vagal Baseline.

It is ultimately what gives your kids the same thing!

If you want to pass down healing and self-connection, and you've skipped doing the practices in the last chapter... gentle reminder that doing your own work is the most important step.

And this chapter on understanding your child's nervous system is going to show you exactly why!

Let's take another breath and contemplate a few regulating thoughts at the same time to get grounded and ready for this chapter. When we've taught parents this content, they often say...

"This information has come at the exact right time," "I feel like I have been calling this in; it's exactly what I need to hear," and *"I don't know how I ended up here learning this, but I feel like it's divine timing."*

So, as an antidote to the pressure you might be subconsciously placing on yourself to quickly and urgently fix your kids' nervous systems (we see you!), let's take another deep breath and just affirm for a moment that whatever is happening within your family nervous system, you are in the right place, at the right time, creating what you need for your kids and your personal well-being.

And exhale! Let's learn more about your child's nervous system!

Your Child's Nervous System

There is one absolutely key difference between an adult's and a child's nervous system:

Children cannot regulate their nervous systems on their own.

This is so profound, and so key to understanding our kids' behavior (especially the tricky ones!), that it bears repeating: *children cannot regulate their nervous systems on their own.*

Throughout childhood and into early adulthood, with still-developing nervous systems, growing humans need to borrow the maturity of the adult nervous system around them in order to regulate.

Another important difference: *What is perceived as threatening to a child is often very small and insignificant for an adult.* Kids are completely vulnerable and dependent on other people for survival, and what is threatening for them is likely to seem like a total non-issue for us! This means kids can be dysregulated for things that can seem like no big deal!

These two things have massive implications for our day-to-day experience of parenting! Let's understand the developing ANS so we can understand our kids (and our inner child!) better!

This will help you to find patience to respond to your child the way you really want to when they aren't listening to you, or are having big feelings, because when you understand their nervous system, you really do know that they are doing the best they can with what they've got!

First, the science . . .

Your Child's Nervous System

Our nervous system is most sensitive in the first months of life when it is starting to form. In this chapter, we are going to go back to the very beginning, so you can really understand just how fundamental the ANS is for our human experience.

You may not be aware of this, but the ANS is one of the first things to start developing in utero. Very, very soon after conception occurs, the rapidly dividing cells form an embryo, and the *neural plate*—a flat group of cells that will develop into the nervous system—emerges. Over the first weeks of pregnancy, this plate folds and closes into the *neural tube*, a structure that will eventually become the brain and spinal cord, marking the beginning of the central nervous system (CNS). These neural cells start to differentiate into various aspects of the ANS, including the sympathetic and parasympathetic systems and the heart.

That's right, within the first few weeks of our baby's physical life, the foundations of their nervous system have already begun to take shape.[1]

And all this can happen before we are aware they have been conceived!

In the first four weeks, while the embryo is only just starting to grow, its development is intrinsically connected to and influenced by its parents. These first cells carry a genetic blueprint from each parent, which holds the embryo's potential and guides the first steps of growth. The environment that the embryo develops within has an influence on which of these genes are silenced and which are expressed.[2] And all of these first moments—that impact the whole of our life—happen in relationship with the outside world via our mother's body and nervous system through changes such as variations in the blood flow, oxygen levels, and nutrient availability,[3] our mum's physiological health, and the emotions and stress levels in our family, which are also influenced by the social and cultural context we have been conceived within.

And it is not a one-way relationship! Mothers are obviously completely changed by a pregnancy; the new embryo's hormonal presence creates changes in its mother's brain and immune systems within days of conception alone.[4] Right from the beginning of our lives, there is a complex, interwoven, multifaceted co-creation between our ANS and the people around us and our environment; in fact, interconnection is our very foundation, with the ANS serving as the first thread that weaves us into the fabric of our relationships and surroundings.

By five or six weeks, our baby's heart starts to beat, and this early rhythm is a much-anticipated milestone, kickstarting the ANS's dance of regulating vital functions.[5] While we are reflecting on sentimental milestones in the womb (how sweet is this!) . . . in the next few weeks are when a baby in the womb practices breathing! From about 11 weeks old, babies take irregular practice breaths every now and then to help prepare their lungs for breathing once they are born.[6] The practice breathing becomes deeper and more regular as birth approaches to prepare the baby for its first breath.

Just like adults, when babies in utero are stressed, they have high levels of sympathetic activity, and when they are relaxed, they have higher levels of parasympathetic activity; although, because the sympathetic nervous system develops the earliest, they are often higher in sympathetic activity in Trimester 2, and more balanced between the two ANS branches by Trimester 3.[7]

Now you might be wondering what on earth would stress out a baby before they are born? How can they even be aware of what is happening around them, let alone be stressed out by it?

And maybe it will come as a surprise to hear that babies are highly sensitive to what is happening around them, even when they are in the womb. They respond to internal and external changes in their environment, like touch, familiar sounds;[8] they can taste and show preferences for specific flavors;[9] they can stretch, kick, and suck their thumb, often moving in response to interactions from people outside the womb;[10] they are light sensitive and might move away from bright lights shone on their mum's belly; and they learn and remember things.[11] Their reactions to things they find stressful (like loud, unfamiliar sounds and bright lights) are reflected in increases in their heart rate and increased, sharper movements. It takes them longer than an adult to regulate back to a parasympathetic state, especially prior to the third trimester, when their nervous system is still sympathetically dominant.[12]

However, a baby in the womb is not confined to their own individual sensory experience.

In utero there is a continual sound of their mother's rhythmic breath, her heartbeat, her blood pulsing around her body, the pace of which all changes as she feels relaxed, happy, satisfied, or heightened with excitement, anger, or fear. And a still-emerging area of research has found evidence of the "coupling" of a baby's heart rate with their mother's heart rate, suggesting that even in utero there are many moments of shared autonomic synchrony,[13] and possibly the beginnings of the "psycho-biologically" attuned attachment relationship.[14] It seems that shared emotionally attuned experiences begin much earlier than we might have thought. A study that measured a mother's heart rate when she did an anxiety-producing task found that when a mother is anxious, her nervous system experiences a sympathetic spike and an increase in her heart rate, and her baby experiences the same increased heart rate.[15] Another research study found that when mothers practice rhythmic, deeper-than-usual breathing, their babies' heart rates lower to synchronize with their mothers' more relaxed states.[16] This suggests that when a mother's heart rate speeds up from stress, emotions, or exercise, so does her baby's, and when she relaxes and her breathing slows and her heart rate stabilizes, again, so does her baby's. These "coupling" moments appear to happen mostly in moments of heightened activation in both the sympathetic nervous system and the parasympathetic nervous system, as opposed to being linked all the time.

Nervous System Coupling

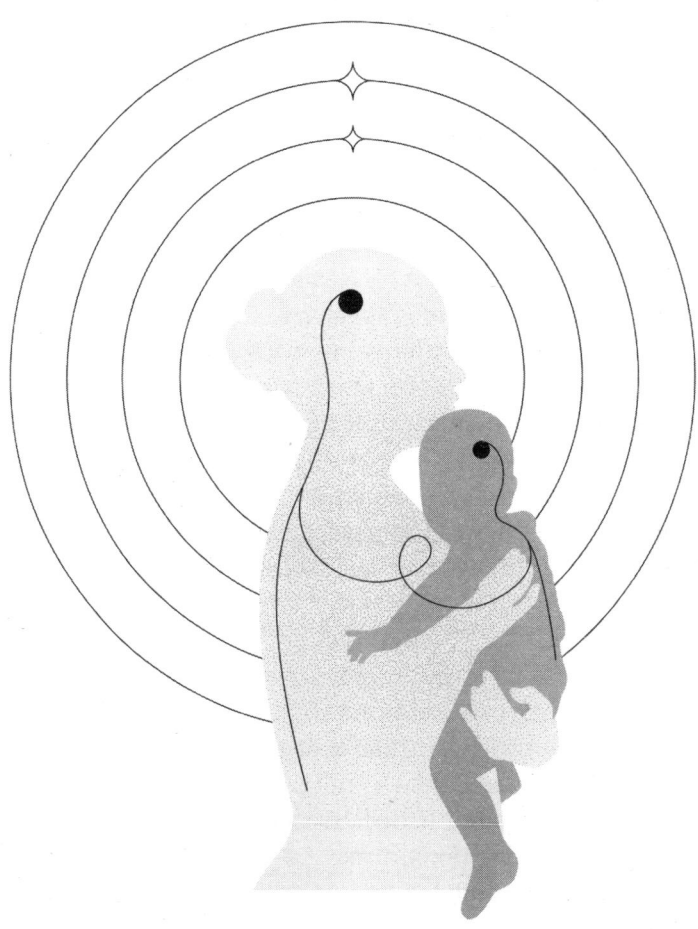

This area of research is still emerging, but like us, you might also enjoy watching the science gradually revealing evidence for what mothers have sensed for probably millennia. Given that in the first year of life outside the womb, emotional and physiological synchrony and shared emotional states form the basis of a strong attuned attachment,[17] why would this connection not exist on some level prior to birth?

Let's take a moment and reflect on your own experience for a moment with your own sense of connection with your kids or with your own parents.

What have you experienced in connection with your babies in utero, or even prior to conception?

Many mothers share stories of having a deep intuitive sense of connection with their babies. Many mothers say they have a feeling about who their babies are, can sense them before conception, or have profound experiences with their unborn baby that open them to the reality that there is a spiritual connection at play. Moments before one of my sons was conceived, I had a glimpse of a curly blond-haired boy and got a sense that he was asking me if he could be conceived! I was taken aback, as I had never had a visual like this before (let alone while making love!), but I also said yes, and sure enough, a month later, I discovered I was pregnant, and a year or so later, he was absolutely the blond curly-headed boy who was the epitome of that vision.

What has been your experience of connection and synchrony with your babies or parents from womb time? You might have a very spiritual experience or may prefer the scientific focus, and both are valid!

Regardless of your perspective, one thing science knows for sure is that having optimal ANS health and a healthy At-Rest Baseline high in parasympathetic activity (which, let's remember, is inextricably linked to the degree that it can predict our emotional and mental well-being) is the most optimal environment for a baby's developing nervous system. Research shows multiple long-term, positive impacts for our children when our optimal nervous system is the foundation of the development of their own nervous system,[18] and it seems to predict the quality of the ease in connection and emotional synchrony after birth as well! Meaning, babies whose mums have a high baseline of parasympathetic activity will have a similarly high level themselves in the years to come, and they will find it easier to emotionally synchronize as a pair in the first days and weeks of their relationship outside the womb.[19]

When does the ventral vagal system develop?

By the time your baby is ready to be born, usually anywhere from around 38 to 42-ish weeks from conception (unless they are born premature or later than expected), their ANS is fully functioning but *nowhere* near fully mature—in fact, it will still be decades before their nervous system reaches full development! As the baby prepares for birth, a very critical development is about to happen. In the last few weeks before the baby is born, there is an especially big increase in development of the parasympathetic nervous system.[20] The vagus nerve becomes *myelinated*. During myelination a protective layer forms around the nerve that allows electrical impulses to move quickly between the nerve cells. This determines how quickly and effectively the vagus nerve can communicate to other parts of the CNS to put the brake on the stress responses. The timing of this surge of maturation in the vagus nerve and parasympathetic branch makes a lot of sense when we think about what a huge, complex transition birth is for mum and baby!

In its innate, ancient, evolutionary wisdom, the ANS is perfectly ready with an effective and speedy rest-and-relaxation response for regulating through the momentous change in environment from warm, supportive, intrauterine life through the birth canal and the birth process to life outside the womb, where we need to quickly learn to breathe, adjust to gravity, and experience light, sound, and all manner of stimulation without the buffer of our warm, watery, safe womb space that has been all we have ever known.

At birth, a baby is suddenly required to do many things on their own: They need to breathe, their heart must beat to circulate their own blood (which was previously done by the placenta), they need to signal hunger and other needs by crying, and more! The very basics of regulating their body is about all they can manage on their own. Other than this, they are completely dependent upon their caregivers to survive. And so, there is a critical aspect of their nervous system that is ready to help them adjust to life outside the womb so they can survive.

Their vagus nerve, the core of the social nervous system, has undergone rapid growth and myelination for this very moment. They are primed for human connection. Their nervous system is already deeply attuned to their mother's voice, heartbeat, and nervous system. This means they are ready to look for faces and eye contact, even in the first moments after birth. They recognize their mother's, father's, and other family members' voices so that they can bond with their carers immediately.

They need to, for survival.

They cannot regulate anything beyond the simplest physiological basics on their own. If they get too hot, their nervous system is not even mature enough to sweat to cool themselves down. To regulate even this basic need, they will need to cry to elicit help from their caregivers.

And so, babies arrive hardwired for relationships—connection is a survival need, right from their first moments.

Deep breaths—let's just let this all digest for a moment.

What happens when a baby has a fright or there is a threat? Think about the way a newborn responds if they are exposed to something like a sudden loud noise, such as a door slamming or a car horn. Their ANS responds very quickly! Have you seen the way a frightened baby will suddenly extend their arms and legs outward in panic, often with a quick cry, as if reacting to a sudden shock? This is known as the startle reflex. When a newborn is startled, this activates the sympathetic branch of the ANS, which causes the heart rate to accelerate and the breathing to speed up to prepare the body for a potential threat. They can respond to threats very effectively, *but,* once they are activated, they cannot come back to balance on their own. To regulate back into their resting state, they will need to borrow the safe, present, loving, and mature nervous system of their caregiver. They will need to be rocked, spoken to in soothing voices, sung to, carried around, and held close to someone to come back to their Reconnected Baseline of ventral vagal.

Babies are completely helpless and dependent on the adults around them for their survival. If they are frightened or shocked, they startle (as above), but if no one is there or no one responds to them, they might stop crying after a while. This can give the impression they have calmed themselves down or that they are okay. In fact, they have likely given up, and the dorsal vagal immobilization has been activated in order to shut down and immobilize their initial sympathetic survival response.[21] The nervous system and our survival responses are very much active from birth; however, they are completely dependent upon others to co-regulate physically and emotionally.

Over many, many thousands of small, daily repetitions of a "bigger, stronger, wiser and kind" adult helping them regulate back to a Parasympathetic Baseline,[22] as their nervous system develops in maturity, children can gradually do this regulation dance on their own.

Yet something deeper is happening in these formative years of extreme nervous-system sensitivity; babies are laying the foundation of their sense of self in a much more profound way than we might realize.

The Sensitivity of a Newborn Nervous System

Did you know that it was only in 1988 that the American Medical Association declared there was enough research to confirm that infants do experience pain?[23] Yep, scary but true: the old paradigm view that babies are born tabula rasa, a blank slate ready to be impressed upon by the world, was not so long ago!

A new paradigm recognizes that babies arrive in the world after birth with their own autonomic signature, made up of all that they have experienced in utero and during birth, as reflected in their unique autonomic balance present at birth.

Despite the newness of a newborn baby, they are not truly "new" in the way that in the past babies have been viewed: they are highly sensitive and attuned to everyone in their environment, and they already have a foundation of rich learning experiences.

The idea that a baby brings their life experience from the womb can be a hard thing for people to accept.

Many people understandably think, *"Well, I can't remember what it was like as a baby, and I have no memories from that time, so I mustn't have been very aware of what I was experiencing at that time either."* In fact, many people today still think or relate to kids as though they won't remember things that happen to them or around them.

It is absolutely true that babies don't remember their experiences in the same way that an adult does.

They don't remember the who, what, when, and where of situations and events. This type of autobiographical memory—like a memory of how it was to go to your first day of school, what it felt like, what school it was, what the teacher's name was—memories like this are called explicit memories, and they don't begin to form until about two years of age.[24]

Your Child's Nervous System—Eleanor

We have mistaken the absence of explicit memories to mean babies and even toddlers are not sensitive to their environment, and what happens to them doesn't matter.

Even though a baby may not have explicit memories, their early experiences are deeply embedded in the body through a different type of memory—implicit memory.

This is where the limbic system of their brain plays a crucial role. The limbic system, which includes the amygdala and hippocampus, is responsible for processing emotions and forming these implicit memories, which are stored as emotional and sensory experiences.

These early memories are not stored as conscious thoughts but instead as feelings in the body. For example, if a baby frequently experiences stress, these sensations are remembered in their nervous system and are reactivated when they experience a similar-feeling situation again (much the same as when we experience a trigger as an adult; see Chapter 6). This complex interaction between the limbic system and the ANS is not just about survival; it's also about how we learn, remember, and emotionally respond to the world around us.

For example, babies quickly learn how their cries are responded to. Babies cry to communicate when they have a need, like hunger, or when they are frightened or upset so as to elicit the support they need to regulate. A baby who is responded to with loving, consistent care that meets their needs will quickly learn that life is safe, they are good, and people are predictable and loving. These implicit memories stay with us, embedded in our limbic memory, activated by the ANS into adulthood, as body memories and working models or Core Beliefs about ourselves, our needs, and other people.[25]

In fact, this might come as a surprise, but we get most of the Core Beliefs about ourselves, life, and other people from how the adults around us related to us and our needs in the first months of life when we were highly dependent and wired for survival.

Our implicit memories become who we feel we are later in life: our sense of self.

They are not conscious memories, but they are evident in every moment of our life in more subtle and all-encompassing ways.

Here is an example of how Reidy got in touch with implicit memories from her prenatal implicit self.

"Going into the breathwork session, I was apprehensive and feeling very aware of my current struggles in life with the kids and in relationships.

"For a long time in the breathwork sessions, I was just feeling annoying pains in my body, and I felt really stuck with it all. For months I felt like I would just lie there thinking there is something wrong with me for not being able to change the way I respond to my kids in life. There are so many areas of my life I feel bad about, that create pain for me, and that make me feel like I am doing life wrong.

"Sometimes this feeling of not being able to change anything in my life gets all too much and I cry, and while that feels good for a while, now I am even feeling annoyed with myself about that. Crying about it isn't changing anything, but recently, I had an experience where this all came to a head and there was a breakthrough.

"I was feeling the same old feelings of physical pain, this pinching in my shoulders, and an immense feeling of being stuck in life. Again, I got to the point of crying that it would never change, when I suddenly had this new thought: What if even though this all feels very true right now, what if like they say, this is actually a body memory of a time when I was little?

"The moment I felt open to relating differently to what was happening in the breathwork session, something opened up for me.

"I could see, or more like 'sense,' this little baby—tiny and stuck in the birth canal. It was me, pinched and tense in my shoulder

blades—in the exact same position I was in in the breathwork session—and I could see I was in the same pain.

"I realized that as a baby in the birth canal, I had disliked that experience of pain and stuckness so much, and from my limited perspective at the time, where there was no separate 'I,' I could identify only with what was happening; because I thought that something was wrong, this meant that I was wrong. And because I disliked what was happening, I disliked myself.

"I realized at that moment: I thought I was the pain. I was stuck. I was wrong. And I could not experience myself in any other way.

"Pain, wrongness, and stuckness became my identity! It is who I thought I was!

"I decided at that time, 'I am wrong,' 'Life is painful,' 'I am stuck and don't like myself,' and it continued to be true for me even as an adult. Even though I don't consciously think about those things, I feel them in my body constantly every day.

"This experience of regressing to the infant psyche, to being pure awareness, to a time when I was so little that I completely identified with the body sensations and with what was happening to me, with no adult reflective capacity at all—just pure experiencing and pure somatic awareness—this small glimpse into the infant psyche, well, it was profound for me.

"Everything that had been coming up for the last months was this body memory of the time when I locked in these beliefs! And it went way further back than I thought, to before I was born!

"And so my next thought was, 'If I'm not the pain, then what am I?'

"I still had a visual of a baby, this soft, innocent, tiny baby, and I felt so much compassion and love and tenderness toward myself, like I never have before!

"I asked the baby me who I was before I made the decision that I was wrong and not to like myself.

"And in the question was the answer: 'I am pure love.'

"And in that moment, I saw this circle, this cycle of love flowing from me now as an adult, capable of holding and healing and softening, flowing into that baby of pure being and raw experience.

"This was big for me, because for a long time I have been hypercritical of myself and playing out the belief that 'I can't,' 'something is wrong with me,' 'I am pain, life is painful,' and the biggie, 'I don't like myself.'

"I now see where all of these stuck places in my life came from, and that they are ultimately not the truth of who I am or how I need to think about myself."

Profound, huh? Just allow the story and this conversation to digest while you take a slow inhale. Let any awareness arise. Stay open!

Okay, so I'm guessing you are wondering what determines what we store as a survival decision like Reidy did, and how do we make sure our kids have implicit memories of being loved and cared for?

When babies have a consistent and good enough carer to help them ground back to safety, not only does their nervous system develop the capacity to self-regulate—by internalizing the patterns of regulation that they experienced with their caregiver as they mature—but their sense of self is based on the experience of being seen, heard, understood, and deemed important!

We have worked with enough parents by now to know that at this point you are likely feeling (1) guilty for your kid's life experience up until now, (2) anxious to know exactly what to do to make sure your kids have the perfect childhood from now on, or (3) triggered about your own childhood experiences.

So let's take a moment and slow your breath down, and then dive into the next chapter, which is all about what our kids really need from us.

CHAPTER 11

How Do I Help My Kids to Regulate?—Eleanor

I have learned, however, that realness, or genuineness, or congruence—whatever term you wish to give it—is a fundamental basis for the best of communication.

— CARL ROGERS

Remember how we said kids can't regulate their nervous systems alone? And that they need to borrow mature nervous systems to regulate?

This is co-regulating.

Think back to Chapter 4, Understanding Our Nervous Systems. Remember the story about the boy in the river who needed saving? I got such a shock when I was the only person who realized he was struggling to swim!

Well, after I knew for sure he was safe, I went and sat back down with my friend. I was relieved, and no longer in active hyperarousal, but still shaky and in disbelief about what I had seen. "It happened so quick," I said to her over and over.

I told her what had happened for me, moment to moment. "I heard this sound that just made me stand up and look over, and then I saw him! No one else was looking." She was transfixed by my story, she listened to every word I said, and as she empathized with what a big experience it was for me, bit by bit, the shaking stopped, and I felt more and more grounded.

Soon enough I felt complete, and we moved on to chatting about other things.

She had helped me to regulate back to ventral vagal—she had co-regulated with me!

You know the feeling of having an issue in life, and how much better you feel after sharing it with someone? That feeling of relief through being seen, heard, and your experience understood is co-regulation, and we all need it!

But there is a myth about co-regulation in the conscious and gentle parenting circles. One that we are going to bust in this chapter.

It is a myth that keeps parents feeling guilty, like they're failures or thinking that they're damaging their kids. It's a myth that keeps parents up at night promising to themselves that they will do things differently next time, because they have lost their temper.

It is a myth that creates internalized shame, that leads to regret, and that keeps parents stuck in a cycle of self-criticism and feeling not good enough.

It is a myth that keeps us striving for "perfect" parenting, feeling like we need to be the gentlest, loving, kind, present parent—all the time.

It is the myth that co-regulating means being calm!

We've spoken to thousands of parents over the years, and almost every single one believes or has experienced some version of the following: If I can stay calm, my kids will stay calm.

We have heard it all . . .

"I feel so guilty when I get frustrated with my daughter even though I know logically I'm just experiencing a basic human emotion."

"I have read so many parenting books and articles that say to stay calm and your kids will do what you say, but I feel like such a failure as a parent that I can't do it consistently."

How Do I Help My Kids to Regulate?—Eleanor

"I've been seeing so much on gentle parenting, and though I respect it, it just doesn't seem realistic all of the time. It makes me feel so bad at the end of the day, and I just don't know if it's ever going to be me! I feel like my kids are doomed!"

Do any of those sentences resonate for you? Have you ever wished you could be calmer more often? Or felt guilty after losing your temper? These thoughts stem from the myth about our nervous systems that to be regulated is to be calm.

It is a myth about co-regulating that if we want to help our kids to calm down, all we need to do is to stay calm ourselves. *Simple, right?* Wrong.

Anyone who has tried to stay calm while waiting for their calmness to rub off on a toddler who is having big feelings about sharing a toy, or who is gritting their teeth waiting for their angry teenager to accept they aren't allowed to go to a party—basically any parent who has tried hard to stay calm while their kids are dysregulated, angry, or upset—will tell you it doesn't really work like that.

What happens when we try to be calm all the time?

To begin with, the first time our child has a tantrum or big feelings, or if we are inspired enough from reading a calm parenting meme, we might even genuinely have the capacity to stay calm.

Sometimes it works smoothly, but most of the time, in order to stay calm, we will need to suppress or push down some of the feelings of irritation or stress we feel about whatever our child is upset about. Let's face it, the reality is kids can have big feelings about lots of things, lots of times a day, and often at the most inconvenient moments!

I mean, let's be real for a second: Do any of you feel genuinely and authentically calm when your kids scream as you are trying to pay for your groceries at the supermarket?

Usually it will activate a trigger or be overwhelming due to the pressure and stress of the moment, but even when we have the capacity to be with the big emotions, we will still not "stay calm" by the definition of what it is to truly co-regulate.

Usually when parents report back that they have stayed calm in this sort of situation, they will describe it like this: "I *managed* to stay calm," or if they didn't succeed, they might say, "I *tried* to stay calm, but I was so overwhelmed that I couldn't."

If you have to bite your tongue or push down irritation in order to feel calm, first of all, there is a very important role these feelings are trying to play in helping you to co-regulate (we will go into this in the Whole Family Nervous System section), and secondly, by suppressing feelings, you are setting them aside and storing the stress in your system to feel later.

Now, the problem is, there is very rarely a time for us to feel those feelings later.

Life is busy, and very few of us are equipped with practices to release and feel stress after it has passed. And so, what happens for most parents is that they suppress their feelings, trying to be calm, until . . . they either explode (the Yeller), not know what to do (the Avoider), want to run away (the Hustler), or try and make the other person feel better (the Pleaser), or a mix of all four!

Which of these is you?

After the Stress Archetype is activated, the next thing that happens is we tend to blame.

This means we blame our kids or the circumstances for making us feel the way we do. We might blame the circumstances, muttering to ourselves something like, "If only the supermarket didn't have those damn lollies in the aisle right near where we have to pay."

Or we blame our kids, thinking things like, *"My child is so stubborn. If they would just be more easygoing,* then *I could stay calm,"* or you might find yourself feeling righteous and saying to your kids, "You should have listened before I lost my cool," or telling yourself, "They were so rude, and so I had no choice but to react that way."

Or we might blame ourselves for the way we responded, thinking, "I am the worst parent" or some variation and promising ourselves that we will do better tomorrow, or that next time we will try harder to stay calm!

And so, most parents who are trying to be calm are actually stuck in a suppression/blame cycle.

Suppression/Blame Cycle

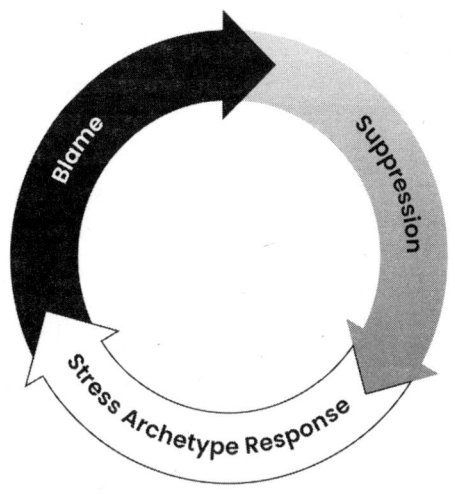

Familiar?

Okay, let's look at the effect that the cycle of trying to stay calm has on our kids, who need us to co-regulate with them.

We discussed that when we try to be calm, we are often suppressing our real feelings, body sensations, and stress responses in order to "be regulated." We do this thinking it will help our kids to stay calm, but it has a different effect from what we think. In reality, we are giving our kids a mixed message.

When our kids are stressed or upset, in our bodies and nervous systems we are generally experiencing subtle to not-so-subtle levels of dysregulation (tension, gritted teeth, nervousness, impatience, or the internalized compassion fatigue eye roll).

Then, as we suppress these feelings, we are putting a mask of calm over the top. We might do this by using a calm voice, smiling, or looking encouraging or empathetic. We may use all the parenting scripts perfectly, naming the emotions, empathizing—we could be absolutely nailing it, being the ultimate calm parent from the outside—and it will make things worse, because there is a more important, louder conversation happening nervous system to nervous system.

Co-regulation is actually an unspoken, body-to-body conversation, in essence.

And because kids pick up what is happening in our nervous systems directly, if we are suppressing a Stress Archetype and trying hard to be calm, what kids actually experience in this moment is confusion, and this confusion generally adds to their dysregulation.

Have you ever noticed that your kids actually escalate when you are trying to feel calm but don't actually feel authentically calm?

It's dysregulating when there is incongruence between what we are saying nervous system to nervous system and what is being outwardly expressed. It can be very confusing for parents when they feel like they are doing the right thing by trying to stay calm, but their attempts to stay calm aren't working for their kids.

I had an epiphany around incongruence when I was in my early 20s. It is strange to think back on now, but I viscerally remember the moment when I realized that people could

How Do I Help My Kids to Regulate?—Eleanor

tell what I was really feeling beneath the words I was saying. I remember having a conversation with my boyfriend and saying—in a voice that I felt was calm—"Sure, go for it," and when he replied, "What is the problem?" it was like he had suddenly held up a mirror. I remember realizing that there was my inner world and my outer world, and they weren't meeting up. I was in denial about the anger I was feeling, and while I thought I was being "chill," I was actually being passive-aggressive. And I was not safe to feel what was really going on for me. And I was totally unconscious of it until I saw it in the mirror. I felt so exposed that I had *honestly* not realized that people could tell how I was feeling below the surface of my response to them.

The most important thing to know is that when we are in denial, or suppressing our emotions, and in a state of incongruence as a result, we are completely disconnected from ourselves!

When kids are presented with this type of incongruence, it is highly dysregulating, because the self-disconnect within their parent's nervous system feels unsafe and confusing. Dysregulated kids don't need us to be calm; they need us to be self-connected and safe to feel what is happening!

There is a cycle that happens to kids when we try to stay calm, but it is incongruent with what is really happening in our emotions and nervous system. It actually escalates their dysregulation.

Masking Cycle

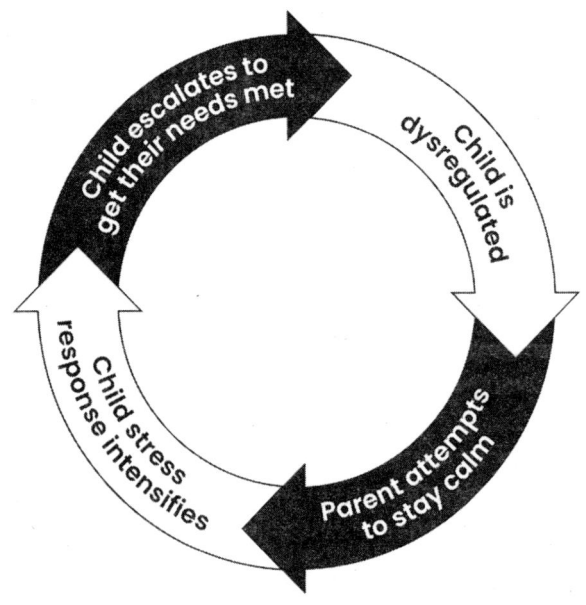

Deep breath! (*Are you beginning to have some ahas about why your calm parenting attempts might not have worked?*)

Then what happens for the parents when their kids are in this cycle? Remember the cycle for the parents above? We try to stay calm, but our kids just escalate, we try to stay calm until . . . we lose it! The Yeller, Hustler, Avoider, or Pleaser comes out in full force!

Either way, we've lost it! We are reactive and have no freedom to choose our responses.

Now, a strange thing can sometimes happen next.

Have you ever lost it, and then *finally* your kids listen. They start behaving or become apologetic.

How Do I Help My Kids to Regulate?—Eleanor

Why?

Well, have you noticed that when we lose it, it can feel like the pressure cooker has burst and we feel relieved on some level also? (This is especially true for Yellers!)

The irony is that congruence and self-connection is so important for regulation that even if it is loud and angry or withdrawn and aloof, it can be more regulating than incongruence and masking—even when that mask is a calm mask!

Except the issue is usually we have acted in ways that we regret and are far from being the parent we want to be.

What is really happening when our kids get dysregulated and they need to borrow our nervous system?

Let's say our child gets hurt, scared, or upset about something. Maybe it comes out of nowhere, or perhaps you've seen it building. Without even thinking, you move toward them—it's instinctual. You scoop them up; your own system gets sympathetically activated as you try to figure out what's wrong. This is the beginning of the co-regulation dance.

At this moment, it's normal and natural for you to feel some dysregulation too. You are alert, concerned, checking for safety. But here's where the magic of a mature nervous system comes in: once you confirm everything is actually safe, you can begin the process of grounding yourself. This might happen naturally, or you might need to take a conscious moment to regulate.

From this more grounded place, you can truly meet your child where they are. Your voice naturally lowers; your touch becomes soothing; you find words to name what they're experiencing. You're transmitting two vital messages: "Yes, this is big!" and "I've got you; it's safe."

Co-regulation isn't about being perfectly calm. It's about being authentic to what is happening within your body and around you while maintaining a sense of groundedness.

Two things often get in the way of us being able to do this.

1. Trying to force ourselves to be "calm" instead of authentic (our kids can feel the difference!), which means we actually end up in a suppression/blame cycle that we outlined above, which more often than not means our kids don't calm down.
2. Being unable to tolerate certain emotions ourselves, making it impossible to stay with these same emotions in our children.

The truth is, co-regulation isn't meant to feel calm, serene, and peaceful. It's meant to feel real, connected, and grounded. Saying that co-regulation is "loaning kids our calm" isn't quite it either.

Have you ever told a friend about something big that happened to you, whether it's a big, exciting thing, or you are sharing sad or hard news? If their response is totally calm, does it feel like they've really understood what has happened? No! You are waiting for them to say, "What? Oh my god!" because they're with you! And what does it feel like to be understood like this? It is very regulating!

Co-regulation starts when we "feel felt" by someone else! We are having a shared emotional experience.

Just imagine that the friend we told our news to stayed neutral and calm, or worse, they got uncomfortable or triggered by your emotions. As adults we'd probably look for someone else to tell, someone who will "get it." Kids can't usually do this; they are reliant on us as their caregivers.

Remember: we can only easily help our children regulate the emotions we're safe to feel ourselves.

Becoming safe to feel our own body sensations and emotions—by giving ourselves the time to see, hear, and understand the suppressed and unintegrated emotions we hold—means that we will be better able to do this dance of co-regulating with our kids. If you get triggered by your kids' needs or emotions, this is an area where you can apply the Reconnected Breath process from Chapter 9 too.

Co-Regulation Cycle

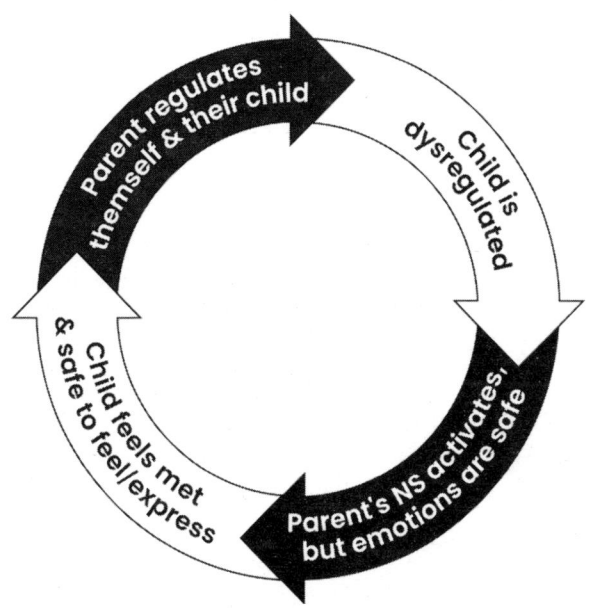

Kids Internalize Our Nervous System

Our kids need to co-regulate with us thousands of times before they can do it themselves. They will embody our capacity to regulate. The things we say become their inner dialogue—they will internalize your voice, and over time and as they develop their own nervous-system maturity, they will be able to self-regulate thanks to your efforts.

At this point, you are probably wondering: How long does it take for your kids to be able to self-regulate? You might be shocked to know that our nervous system doesn't mature until we are close to 30 years old! Yep!

But don't freak out—in the next chapter, we will outline the gradual maturing of the nervous system into adulthood and what we need across childhood.

First, though, this dance of co-regulation has another effect, especially within the first 1,000 days of your child's life, when they are most dependent upon us and when they are right-brain dominant.

The breathwork philosophy is that when we are little, helpless, and dependent on our caregivers, we get impressions about ourselves, life, and relationships that are locked into our body memory—and these stay with us for life. We internalize the impressions we receive, and these become our lifelong working model about "what life is" and "who we are" and "what we can expect from others."

Think back to Reidy's experience in Chapter 10: as an infant she experienced pain, and she couldn't change it, and she decided, "I am wrong" and "life is painful." It was completely true and valid at the time, but living out that decision as an adult was extremely limiting.

Our impressions are not always negative; we receive positive impressions also. For example, if a baby experiences an unmet need, they don't have the maturity to decide, "Oh, my caregiver is just in the next room and will be back in a minute"; they experience aloneness and decide, "I am alone" or similar. When their caregiver returns in response to their cries, they may then experience "I am heard," "I matter," and "I am loved." When responsive caring happens again and again, it can disconfirm negative impressions.

How Do I Help My Kids to Regulate?—Eleanor

You see, for the first two years of life, we are right-brain dominant. Allan Schore's work suggests that it is during these years that we are internalizing our experiences as our sense of self. He has found that this sense of self is stored in the right brain, which is mostly the limbic system and the brain stem.[1] Based on his neurobiological model, for optimal development of a positive sense of self, during these formative years we need many moments of shared limbic resonance, and right-brain to right-brain relating! What is this?

A psychobiologically attuned relationship happens when there is an accurate tracking and awareness of the child's internal emotional and physical world.[2] This happens through a caregiver's own physical and emotional sensitivity to their child's experience. It is mostly a nonverbal, felt way of communicating. Babies receiving this level of attuned care feel "understood" at a somatic level.

As parents, we spend many hours gazing at our babies, full of love, adoring them. As babies grow, we ideally share many moments of delight and love—smiling, babbling, and genuinely enjoying the connection. During this time, if a baby experiences a subtle overwhelm, an attuned carer will feel even this small change in their emotion and adjust the way they are relating to them accordingly. In the previous chapter, we talked about autonomic coupling, where an infant and parent's heart rate, breathing, and other autonomic functions sync up, and they share a physiological and emotional experience. Having relationships where we feel understood at this psychobiological level means that seamless co-regulating is the foundation of our sense of self.

Can you see how this would give a deeply somatic sense of being "seen, heard, and understood"? Of being loved, important, and worthy? Imagine for a moment the Core Beliefs that would form within this type of caring.

When we spend the first months of our children's life in autonomic harmony and synchrony, we have a solid foundation for co-regulating through big feelings and experiences when they are older.

Limbic Resonance

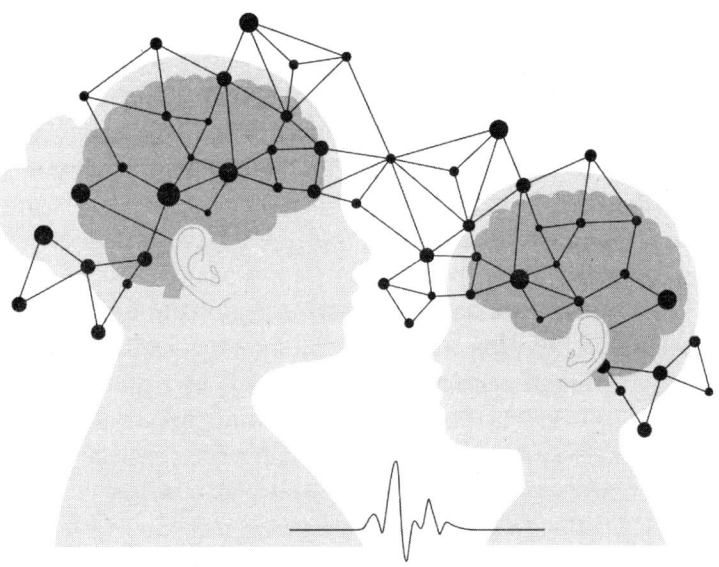

So, a quick pause now—who reading this has decided that they are now going to make sure they are perfectly attuned to their children, 100 percent of the time? Or who is feeling pressure to be the perfect co-regulator?

When you first come to this information, it is common to wonder, what makes my parenting "good enough"? How do I make sure my kids have positive beliefs about who they are? How much attunement is enough?

How Do I Help My Kids to Regulate?—Eleanor

Attachment research shows that we don't need every single need met all the time to feel secure within our relationships to people or in our sense of self. Rather, we need most of our needs met most of the time. Psychologist Edward Tronick found that in healthy, secure relationships, attunement and synchrony happen only about 30 percent of the time. Getting it right 30 percent is "good enough." What happens in the remaining 70 percent is still as important. What makes up the other 70 percent? Ruptures and repairs. When we are misattuned or out of sync with our kids because we are busy, tired, having a bad day, or just not quite noticing or being sensitive to what is happening for them, this is called a *rupture*.

Why are ruptures important? Because they allow for repairs and for learning that it's safe to have moments of imperfect attunement. Micro-moments of unpleasant stress build resilience and ground kids in the reality of being separate individuals. It's not possible for anyone to track our moment-to-moment experience perfectly 100 percent of the time, and as parents we shouldn't strive to give this to our kids.

Ultimately, what we need is someone to stay with our experience in a way that we feel seen, heard, and understood—and with whom we can dance through ruptures and repairs in a way that builds resilience within.

Being there enough of the time is, well, *enough*. Relieved?

What our kids need from us also changes as they mature, so let's look at some basics of regulating throughout the maturation of the nervous system.

CHAPTER 12

When Can My Kids Self-Regulate?

We are co-regulatory, until we no longer need to be co-regulatory.
— STEPHEN PORGES

How long will we need to loan our nervous system to our kids?

Think about the last time you had a really tough day at work or got some overwhelming news. What did you do? If you're like most of us, you probably reached out to someone—maybe called a friend, texted your partner, or dropped by a family member's house. That's your nervous system doing exactly what it's designed to do—seeking connection to help you feel steady again.

We all need signs of safety and human connection to truly come back to optimal, regulated, *self*-connection.

How well we can create this for ourselves as adults is heavily influenced by how consistently other people were there for us when our nervous system was developing! We internalize the nervous system's regulatory capacity of the adults around us—like a blueprint—and then we gradually become more and more masterful at doing it for ourselves as our nervous system develops.

The way our caregivers responded to our distress and celebrated our joy becomes deeply embedded in our nervous system, forming an unconscious internal blueprint for how we regulate in relationships throughout our lives.

And this process of maturing into self-regulation takes longer than you would think!

In fact, our nervous system isn't fully mature till we are 28!

Maturity of the Nervous System

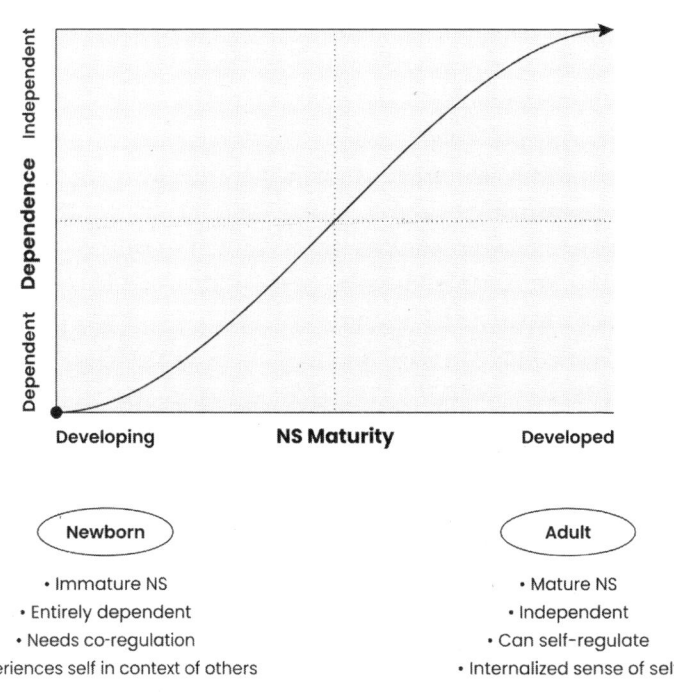

Okay, it's a "deep breath" moment! Hands up if you are freaking out at how long you'll have to regulate your kids for, or maybe you are realizing how young you were when you were independent and didn't have anyone to turn to. But our ability to regulate our nervous system matures as our independence grows; what our kids need from us at birth is different from what they need as a 28-year-old. So, let's go deeper in this to understand what our kids can and cannot regulate for themselves as they are growing up.

Regulating Across the Lifespan

When kids are dysregulated, they are in an overwhelming survival experience that can completely take them over. You will have seen this in toddlers! Their emotions take over their whole body; they throw themselves around, completely swept up in the big feeling! Dysregulation is a big experience for kids, and their ability to regulate depends on their age, their development, their unique individual life circumstances, their autonomic signature and baseline, their current physical state (tired, hungry, or other physical need), their constitution, their neurodivergence, and more.

Dysregulation can be a full-body, out-of-control emotional experience.

Just think about what it is like when something happens that massively triggers you—even as adults, we can feel out of control and be completely overwhelmed with the intensity of an emotion! Even as adults, we can become irrational, make no sense, even to ourselves, and have to work hard to control our emotions—or find that we can't! Staying with the intensity of big feelings is a lot for most people.

Kids feel the same intensity, but without the capacity to regulate, ground themselves down, or think logically or rationally about what is going on, yet often there are high expectations of children and how they should be able to behave when upset or stressed.

Kids also get dysregulated over things that adults might feel that they have "no good reason" to get upset about, because our stress response is about our perception of an event, not about the event itself. What is big to a child will seem totally small to an adult.

We all know how baffling it is when our kids get upset about the color of their cup or the shape their toast was cut!

Let's have a look at how the nervous system develops from in the womb to the full maturity of the nervous system at around age 28, and what they need from you in order to regulate, so we can begin to really land in a new perspective that makes parenting so much easier—*they are doing the best they can with what they've got.*

This information is based on approximate neurotypical development and is focused on regulation—and is not to be used diagnostically. It is for reflections, understanding, and awareness of play in the coming chapters.

The First 1,000 Days (Conception to Age 2)

Central and Autonomic Nervous System Development:

- Babies are sensitive to internal and external stimuli even in the womb, and are getting their first impressions of life and co-regulation experiences in utero.
- The ventral vagus nerve myelinates just before birth, preparing the baby for social connection.
- In the first year is when the baby sees the most rapid growth of the brain and nervous system.
- The parasympathetic branch, especially the ventral vagal complex, matures significantly.

- The baby is beginning to regulate basic functions like heart rate, digestion, and sleep-wake cycles.

Regulation Needs:

- Their nervous system is designed to sync with their caregiver's system.
- Crying is their only way to communicate regulation needs.
- They're completely dependent on co-regulation.
- Their stress responses take longer to settle than adults.
- Even small changes can be overwhelming to their system.
- They need consistent responses to develop a sense of safety.

For example: Newborns are completely dependent on their caregivers, even for regulation of their temperature and basic physical needs. A six-month-old might become overwhelmed by a loud noise and cry inconsolably. This is their nervous system being exactly as sensitive as it needs to be at this age.

Early Childhood (Ages 2–7)

Central and Autonomic Nervous System Development:

- The central nervous system and limbic system undergo a significant growth spurt.
- The right-brain system continues to encode working models of regulation.

- The rational left brain begins development around age two.
- Everyday nervous-system function becomes more balanced between the sympathetic and parasympathetic responses.
- The child can gradually regulate body temperature and basic physical needs.

Regulation Needs:

- Their emotional brain develops faster than their rational brain.
- Big reactions to small things reflect genuine neural overwhelm.
- They can't yet match their emotional response to the size of an event.
- Their regulation needs change rapidly throughout the day.
- What they can handle one day might overwhelm them the next.
- Social and emotional challenges feel as big as adult-sized crises.

For example: A four-year-old's meltdown over a broken cookie isn't an overreaction; to their developing system, it feels like an adult losing a major project at work.

Middle Childhood (Ages 7–14)

Central and Autonomic Nervous System Development:

- The limbic system undergoes another burst of maturation.
- There is significant development in the amygdala and hippocampus.
- A deeper awareness of personal history emerges.
- The ability to see the self as a separate individual develops.
- The beginning of puberty brings hormonal influences on regulation.
- The brain undergoes significant reorganization.

Regulation Needs:

- Children often appear more capable than their nervous systems actually are.
- Their regulation abilities can vary widely day to day.
- Social challenges are processed with intense neural activity.
- They need support handling increased emotional complexity.
- They may experience episodes of regression during stress.
- Puberty impacts emotional stability and regulation needs.

For example: A 10-year-old might move confidently through their weekly routine of school and activities yet become dysregulated and emotional when faced with an unexpected change like a substitute teacher or a canceled sports practice. Their nervous system is developed enough to handle familiar situations but still needs significant support navigating unexpected changes or disappointments.

Adolescence (Ages 14–21)

Central and Autonomic Nervous System Development:

- A significant wave of synaptic pruning begins in the limbic system.
- The prefrontal cortex is still developing.
- Enhanced cognitive functions are developing but not complete.
- Hormonal changes heavily influence the child's regulation capacity.
- Brain reorganization continues throughout this period.

Regulation Needs:

- Their seemingly erratic behavior reflects brain reorganization.
- Emotional reactions are intensified by biological changes.
- The need for independence conflicts with the need for co-regulation.
- Their regulation abilities can seem inconsistent.

- Complex emotions need processing support.
- Social challenges feel especially intense.

For example: Your 16-year-old might make very sensible choices most of the time and then suddenly do something risky and spontaneous without really thinking things through! Their brain's ongoing reorganization means they can appear extremely mature in some moments and need lots of support in others; both responses are perfectly appropriate for their developmental stage.

Young Adulthood (Ages 21–28)

Central and Autonomic Nervous System Development:

- Final stages of prefrontal cortex development
- Increasing "top-down" regulation capacity
- More cognitive control over emotional responses
- Full myelination of major neural pathways
- Integration of emotional and rational processing

Regulation Needs:

- Growing independence while still completing nervous system maturation
- Need for co-regulation during major life transitions
- Support needed for complex emotional experiences
- May still struggle with intense stress responses

- Regulation needs fluctuate with life challenges
- Building capacity for self-initiated co-regulation

For example: Your young adult might be doing really well at their new job, but then they call you in tears about relationship troubles or feeling overwhelmed about whether to take a job in another city. This back and forth between independence and needing support isn't a sign that they're not adulting well—it's actually a sign of healthy development when they are able to reach out for co-regulation and support.

Regressions

It is normal for kids to regress to previously mastered developmental stages when they are going through—or when the adults around them are going through—a stressful period of time, or when they are about to go through a developmental leap.

A very common time to see this is when a new baby arrives in the family, and the older siblings (especially toddlers) regress to baby talk or being more needy around sleep, needing more cuddles, or just being upset more easily in general.

Sometimes this can be interpreted as our kids trying to get more attention or being jealous of the new baby and acting manipulatively.

This could be in part true!

But more importantly, their nervous system is showing us exactly what it needs to feel safe during a big change.

Regression isn't manipulation; it's a natural, adaptive response that helps children integrate new experiences. When kids return to earlier developmental stages, they're instinctively seeking the safety and regulation support that helped them navigate that stage the first time. By meeting these needs without judgment, we help them gather the resources they need to move forward again. Their nervous system knows exactly what it needs to process change and growth, even if it doesn't make logical sense to our adult minds.

Quick Reminders About Regulation:

- Behind every "difficult" behavior is an unmet regulation need.
- Dysregulation is not manipulation; it's communication.
- Children's reactions always make sense from their developmental stage.
- Regression under stress is normal at every age.
- A child who seems "too old" for a reaction is likely experiencing something beyond their current capabilities.
- Regulation needs fluctuate. This isn't going backward; it's part of development.
- When they seem most "difficult," they're often most in need of co-regulation.
- Their nervous system is doing exactly what it should for their stage.
- Big reactions mean they trust you with their big feelings.

Sometimes when we share this information with parents, they realize they had to parent themselves and that they never really had adults with mature nervous systems around them as they were growing up.

The adults around them had physical maturity but lacked emotional maturity and the ability to regulate themselves, let alone their kids! If this is you, you might have taken on responsibility for parenting your siblings or for trying to regulate and make sense of the adults. This can leave you feeling like a serious adult who has high levels of stress and is hyperindependent. This might have happened in the context of "little t" moments of insensitivity that made a big impression on you in some areas of life, or "big T" moments, where you really didn't get what you needed even 30 percent of the time.

The first step in the Reconnected Parenting model is to show up for ourselves in the places where the adults weren't there for us when we were little—this being the adult nervous system we needed at the time. The "staying with" we needed when we were little, we can now give it to ourselves as adults.

"My intention today was healthy boundaries between my mother and I that bring me ease in our relationship and freedom in my life, especially when I'm around her.

"Right off, there was so much anxiety dropping into my body, widespread all over. Like when you're caught somewhere you're not supposed to be or overhear something you know isn't appropriate for you, that kind of awful, heavy feeling, especially in the pit of my stomach.

"As I was sitting with that feeling, it hit me that she always crossed lines like this throughout my life. From sharing too much about her relationship with my dad, to her own childhood traumas, her relationship to her parents, it was all too much for me to hear at that young age, and it brought on overwhelming tears today in the session. So much heavy sadness and pressure in my chest and shoulders and painful tingling in my hands.

"After I stayed with that sensation for a while, a wave of sweeping relief flooded my body.

"I was actually laughing and crying because I realized that I show up for not only me, but for all the women and girls I once was whose boundaries were violated by her, and that they are now being held safely." —Rea, Reconnected community member

When Can My Kids Self-Regulate?

Being an adult means being able to regulate, but it is not the end of our evolution or maturity. There is another step of maturing that is the full expression of our capacity to be available for others, and that is stepping beyond the adult nervous system and into the elder nervous system, which we will share more about in the Whole Family Nervous System section.

First, though, let's understand the Five Kids Stress Archetypes, so we can better understand what our kids might need from us.

CHAPTER 13

The Five Kids Stress Archetypes—Eleanor

Play is the child's symbolic language of self-expression.
— Garry Landreth

I remember the day my strong-willed child threw sand at one of the parents at playgroup. He was two, and I was watching him hogging the swing while I breastfed the newborn baby. Cringing while he ignored the impatiently waiting kids, I moved as quickly as I could toward him while holding the baby (mums of two or more, I know you know this juggle!). I could sense a situation building!

Unfortunately, I didn't get there in time, another mum swooped in, and with a lot of tension, she came right in close to him and said with a kind but stern voice, "No! It's not just yours! You need to share!"

To which my son promptly matched her energy, looked her square in the eye as he reached down to pick up some sand, and said "No!" and then he threw the sand at her. I was a whole mix of horrified at his behavior, annoyed with the other parent, but mostly, at a loss as to why he was so. Dang. Reactive all the time.

Honestly, the humbling situations I've navigated with this kid.

If I didn't have at least *one* empathic, sensitive, mostly compliant kid already . . . I reckon I would have fallen into a pit of despair with this little guy about what a terrible parent I was!

I remember feeling super judged and so apologetic toward the other mum, who was pretty offended.

But the main problem was, I just had *no* idea why he was so hard! Nothing seemed to "work" with him! He was so explosive! At the time (2006!) no one I knew was talking about the nervous system, I had no way to understand what he was needing, and most parenting advice ranged from "just be stricter," "take things away from him when he hits," or some version of "punish him if he does anything wrong."

I didn't realize until many years later he was stuck in fight mode!

We have found that like adults, kids typically have five different Stress Archetypes. In this chapter, we want you to identify your child's Stress Archetype. This is either how they behave *most of the time*, or it might be their reactions triggered in specific situations, and then we are going to use it to understand their Core Beliefs and implicit sense of self.

The Explosive Child

The Explosive child goes from 0 to 100 in a split second. They are often labeled oppositional, defiant, and naughty! The Explosive child is stuck in a Fight response.

The Fight response in kids can look like:

- Yelling and screaming
- Hitting, kicking, throwing, and punching
- Being controlling and demanding
- Being angry and aggressive

The challenge for the parent of the Explosive child:

The Fight response in kids is often the most judged nervous-system response! We may feel judged for their "bad" behavior. Often when our kids explode, there is a panicky feeling of needing to quickly stop their explosive behavior. This feeling can make us reactive and fall into punishment or yelling, but when we do this, we are joining them in the Fight response!

What you need to know about the Explosive child:

Your child has fight! This means they are no pushovers in life, and when they are stressed, they feel they can meet the challenge and take it on! They have not given up. Underneath the reaction is a child who does feel capable and is willing to take on the world. They know they can do something about their situation!

The Anxious Child

The Anxious child is often restless and fidgeting. They can feel chaotic and tense to be around—which is a reflection of their inner world!

The Flight response in kids can look like:

- Anxious, panicked, and scared
- Hyperactive, restless, and fidgeting
- Escaping and running away
- Avoiding issues and hiding away
- Showing up as anxiety

When kids' nervous systems are in this state of Flight, they are actually unable to listen and may appear quite distracted, be restless, and run away. For kids in Flight, it seems like the best option is to get out of the situation as fast as possible in order to survive. Even though there may be nothing that is actually life-threatening, it feels very real to them.

The child is often described as hyperactive with an inability to sit still. It is a state of hyperarousal in their system, and the physical sensations can be quite overwhelming—racing heart, fast breathing, and tense muscles.

The challenge for the parent of the Anxious child:

When our kids avoid us or run away from the issue, it can appear that they are intentionally avoiding getting in trouble. In reality, they are trying to escape feelings and sensations that feel unsafe!

The challenge is to recognize the inner tension that they feel and to help them find ways to soothe this, so that they can arrive and face the present moment.

What you need to know about the Anxious Child:

Anxiousness is often associated with shyness or quietness, but in fact in kids it can look like dominating a conversation so they can get it over quicker. They might yell, "I already know what you are saying" or refuse to listen, or run away. The challenge is to help your child be in the present moment, feeling safe and arriving here without needing to escape.

The Golden Child

The Golden Child is often overlooked. They are the easygoing kids, the ones who are a pleasure to parent, and they rarely rock the boat.

The Fawn response in kids can look like:

- Perfectionism, wanting to get it right
- People-pleasing
- Worrying about everyone else
- Saying sorry a lot and rarely getting angry

The Fawn response is so often overlooked in children, because this child is often described as good, complacent, and a pleasure! But it can be a state of hypoarousal that is hard to spot because these traits are what society values in kids. Things you can watch out for are when they are saying sorry often, showing no anger, or are trying to make others happy.

The challenge for the parent of the Golden Child:

The tricky thing is, the Golden Child is often behaving exactly as society wants children to behave! Your challenge is to look beyond this, to see beyond their good behavior, and to help them to express what is underneath it, without fear of upsetting others.

What you need to know about the Golden Child:

Your child will suppress their emotions, or maybe even not be in touch with them, because they are so oriented to making sure they don't upset other people. Your role as a parent is to help them to get in touch with their truth beneath the hypoarousal of the Fawn response.

The Dreamy Child

The Dreamy Child can seem like they are in their own world a lot of the time, and then when they are upset, they whine, whinge, get stuck, and aren't open to solutions.

The Freeze response in kids can look like:

- Holding their breath
- Shutting down
- Whining
- Unable to move
- Doesn't answer you
- Saying, "I don't know" a lot

If you are noticing these behaviors in your child, there is a chance they are experiencing a Freeze response. The Freeze response is a state of hypoarousal in their nervous system. For your child, the Freeze response can feel to them like "I don't know what's going on"; they will often be unable to name their feelings, daydream a lot, and say, "I don't know" often.

The challenge for the parent of the Dreamy Child:

It can be highly frustrating for the parent of the child who is dreamy—they don't listen. They avoid eye contact; they shut down; they refuse to answer you!

They get stuck, and we often feel at a loss, helpless, and infuriated. The more we try to help, the more they say, "I don't know." The challenge is to create the time and space they need to get back into motion.

What you need to know about the Dreamy Child:

The Freeze response is like having one foot on the brake and one foot on the accelerator—in equal measure! It's highly charged but immobilizing all at once. Often parents feel frustrated, upset, and annoyed that they cannot get their child to listen and do what they are being asked! It seems so simple from the outside looking in!

And of course, there is the Reconnected Child.

The Reconnected Child

The Reconnected Child is anchored to their ventral vagal state.

This is the child who is safe to feel and express themselves and who feels safe, seen, heard, and understood for who they are. They have Stress Archetype moments, but they are in the context of what is happening around them. They spend most of their time feeling Reconnected.

The Reconnected Child expresses their sense of safety by:

- Whistling
- Singing
- Playing independently
- Showing you things they are excited and proud about
- Hearing and following requests
- Grounding down after upsets and big feelings
- Caring about themselves and others

Which Stress Archetype is my child?

Your child will naturally flow between all of these archetypes in life.

Ideally, they will spend much of their time Reconnected, and then their bodies will activate a Stress Archetype when there's something happening around them that makes them feel unsafe, uncertain, or pressured in some way or a situation triggers or reactivates something from the past for them.

With an adult to co-regulate with, they will come back to the Reconnected Archetype once that threat has passed. They get stressed, but they will quickly return to their Reconnected Baseline. If this sounds like your child, ask yourself:

- How often is my child in a Reconnected state?
- What Stress Archetype is their "go-to" when stressed?
- What are the triggers?

However, like adults, many children have a hard time returning to their baseline! We start writing our autonomic signature at conception, and our nervous system holds the imprint of our entire life experience, so even small children and babies can carry stored stress and spend more time in Stress Archetypes or struggle to return to their baseline.

Some questions to ask yourself to see if this is *your* child:

- Which Stress Archetype does your child spend most of their time in?
- How often are they in that state?
- What is their baseline?
- When do they Reconnect to themselves? What is happening around them at those times?

You might also see a few of the Stress Archetypes in your child's behavior, and many parents ask us, "Can my child be a mix?" And, like adults, yes, you can be multiple Stress Archetypes.

Let's explore this by reflecting which environments bring out which Archetype in your child. Maybe they are the Golden Child at school, but at home they are the Explosive Child. This would suggest that at home they are able to feel capable and like they can do something to change the circumstances that stress them out with their Fight response, but at school they might have given up on that and have found safety in complying and giving up their personal needs and voice. To discover which is true for your child, ask yourself:

What environments bring out which Stress Archetype in my child?

What do our kids' Stress Archetypes tell us about their Core Beliefs?

When our kids are in a Stress Archetype, it can tell us a lot about their Core Beliefs; here's why. Core Beliefs are made at a time when we were little, helpless, and completely dependent; they're based on unconscious survival decisions. Remember that when we're little, we're completely dependent on others, which makes our ANS extremely sensitive, and at the same time, we are developing our sense of who we are.

And these Core Beliefs aren't stored like conscious thoughts—they exist as implicit memories, as a somatic-emotional felt sense.

Because these survival decisions were made when we were helpless and dependent, we'll do everything we can to avoid reexperiencing the feelings we had in that moment. This is why we have such a low tolerance to circumstances that activate our Core Beliefs—because the Core Beliefs are based on decisions we made when we were in survival mode.

Whenever our kids start to have an experience that confirms their Core Belief, it is highly dysregulating for them; their stress archetype often emerges as an attempt to avoid *reexperiencing that Core Belief as true.*

For example, if I am an Explosive Child with a Core Belief "I'm wrong" and someone looks at me like I've done the wrong thing, I might explode to avoid experiencing the "I am wrong" feeling. Why? Because the belief "I am wrong" was a survival decision at the time, and it felt life-threatening when it was formed. It was a decision I made to cope with what felt like a life-or-death experience, even though I was just a small child trying to make sense of my world.

Having any ahas about your child's Stress Archetype?

Ask yourself, what is the trigger for my child's Stress Archetype? What might this say about their Core Beliefs?

Here is a list of common negative Core Beliefs for each archetype compared to their Reconnected Beliefs:

The Explosive Child

I am too much.	I am capable.
I hurt people.	I am strong.
I am bad.	I make good choices.
I am wrong.	People help me.

The Anxious Child

I am not okay.	I am okay.
Life is too much for me.	I know what is happening.
I can't do it.	I can do it.
I am weak.	I am safe.

The Golden Child

I am responsible for others.	I am safe to be me.
I have to wait.	My timing is perfect.
I can't do what I need.	I am safe as I am.
I am unlovable.	I am perfect as I am.

The Dreamy Child

I am confused.	I can connect.
Life is not clear.	I trust myself.
I am lost.	I have people to organize my feelings.
I can't move forward.	I feel clear.

Now, important sidenote: the worst thing you can do for a child in a Stress Archetype is to talk about your observations. Remember from Chapter 11 what we needed when we were little? We needed right-brain to right-brain, felt-sense, non-verbal, soothing behaviors.

Talking about our kids' patterns or analyzing them is like pushing them away from us right when they need us the most. This can be damaging to our connection with them! Think about how it is for you when you are losing it and your partner or friend says, "Hey, is this a Core Belief playing out?" Oh my, it's even more dysregulating right?

As well, kids do not process best verbally; their natural way to process their experiences and regulate themselves is through play!

But they can't do it alone.

Ready to learn more? Chapter 14 is all about play.

CHAPTER 14

Play Is Regulating —Eleanor

Enter into children's play, and you will find the place where their minds, hearts, and souls meet.

— VIRGINIA AXLINE

When you think about play, you might think of board games, kids dressing up and role-playing, make-believe games, and you might also think that it is just something that kids do for fun.

But play is so much more than this!

One thing has always fascinated me as a play therapist. While adults need to intentionally set aside time to focus on a breathwork process to integrate their stress, children instinctively know how to do this through play.

They have a natural ability to allow their nervous system to unwind, and in fact, all their behavior is an attempt to regulate back to a Reconnected Baseline. It's like they instinctively know what they need to do, say, express, and experience to step back into the Reconnected Archetype—no matter what has happened in life.

Emma's story with her son Halo is the perfect example. She shares:

I'll never forget the day I was dressing Halo, my nine-month-old son, and as he squeezed his head through the jumper, our eyes met, and I said, "There he is!"

He beamed, loving the interaction.

He cracked up laughing and started pulling his head back inside, wanting to do it again. He loved that moment, so we kept doing it over and over—his head popping through the jumper, "There you are!" and the laughter, the connection, the joy just overflowed.

There was something magical about that moment—it felt like it was just the two of us in the room. I was utterly captivated by his radiant smile and his happiness in such a simple but deeply adorable moment.

After years of connecting with my other kids through play, I could sense something very integrating and special was happening for him, although I wasn't sure what.

I'm not sure if I've mentioned this, but having twins was a complete surprise, and they were born at home! I had no idea Halo was there until birth.

Halo's sister, Faedra, was born first. She shot into the world head-first, immediately vocal, crying, and fully expressive, her skin pink and vibrant. My other children were there to witness her birth, and the whole family celebrated, "Yes! It's Faedra, she's here!" We all had a moment to admire and delight in her arrival.

Then, just three minutes later, I had another surge while holding Faedra. Two little feet emerged! The shock—another baby? But instinct took over, and with another surge, out came a little boy. He was limp, blue-gray, and the room grew silent. We had to call this baby into the world! After a few moments of clearing the fluid from his mouth, rubbing his back, and getting him to cry, he finally arrived. But his arrival was completely different from his sister's just minutes earlier.

He didn't arrive with excitement and celebration. Instead, we were shocked and worried about him.

Play Is Regulating—Eleanor

As they got older, their personalities matched their arrival! When they started crawling, Faedra was always moving forward, so confident and determined to explore. Halo, on the other hand, was the opposite. He was shy and often avoided eye contact with people. I had never seen such a shy baby!

When he was trying to crawl, he kept sliding backward. He was frustrated and confused, not understanding why he moved backward and got farther away from things when he was trying to follow Faedra.

Most people might not even notice this, but with my years of experience in breathwork and understanding birth patterns, I recognized that Halo was re-creating his birth pattern. His sister, who came first, was confident and moved forward with ease. But Halo, less confident, seemed unable to find his way.

Despite this realization and my deep connection with him, I didn't know how to support him in moving forward, other than trusting in his own timing and being there for him through his frustration.

Then, I had that most spontaneous, beautiful moment with him as we were playing "There you are!" and celebrating him as he "arrived" through the jumper. He loved it and did it over and over.

While it felt special, I didn't think too much of it at the time and began getting everyone else ready, when suddenly, the big kids started shouting, "Halo's crawling forward!" We all cheered! He was beaming, and from that moment on, he never crawled backward again.

Amazing story, isn't it? It was all possible because Emma knew how to connect and regulate through play. And did you notice she wasn't deliberately facilitating his experience or trying to create an outcome for Halo? He instinctively knew exactly what he needed to do. The perfect example of how kids know exactly what they need to do, say, and experience for themselves to rewire and integrate their experiences in life. Even when they are babies—and all through play!

As renowned play therapist Garry Landreth says, "Play is the child's symbolic language of self-expression and can reveal (a) what the child has experienced; (b) reactions to what was experienced; (c) feelings about what was experienced; (d) what the child wishes, wants, or needs; and (e) the child's perception of self."[1]

Play is as much lying in the grass, watching the clouds go overhead, or exploring rocks in a creek in nature as it is playing a board game or dressing up as a policeman and pretending to catch a robber.

Play is happening when a baby looks at their hands and grasps to reach their caregiver's glasses. Play happens when you are playing chess with your teenagers and everything in between.

Play is how kids learn, grow, and develop, and it is also how they communicate their experiences, understand themselves, and regulate their nervous systems. The way our kids play tells us a lot about our kids' nervous-system state—both their Current State and their Habitual Baseline—as well as their implicit sense of self and Core Beliefs.

Play and the Nervous System

Let's have an embodied experience of the polarity of a child's nervous system through play. This is the play equivalent of the left nostril and the Breath of Fire pranayama we did together to explore our ANS in Chapter 4.

Before diving into the play activity, pause and take a moment to notice your child's Current State. Without interrupting what they are doing (or staring too hard at them!), just take a moment and notice their behavior.

Are they feeling calm, fidgety, or maybe a little restless? Are their movements sharp and quick, or lethargic and slow? Perhaps they are focused and engaged, or maybe they're easily distracted.

Is there an emotion they seem to be experiencing?

Notice their breathing: Is it fast or slow? Does it seem shallow or full? Observe without judgment—just notice.

And take a moment to ask yourself: *What does it feel like in my body to be around them in their Current State?* (We will use this observation in the Whole Family Nervous System section!)

Don't offer your opinion on what they are experiencing at this point, but if it feels fun, and depending on their age, ask them to notice too.

If they are under three years old, you can observe them and mentally make notes to yourself. Kids who are older than a few years old, you might ask them if they would like to play a game, and the first step is to describe how their body feels, whether they feel relaxed, excited, or tired. For younger children, keep it simple: "Are you feeling fast like a race car or slow like a turtle?"

Let's Play! The Freeze and Melt Game

Let's take what we just observed and turn it into a playful activity that mirrors the two main states of the nervous system.

This game is a fun way for you to notice changes in your child's ANS and for your child to physically experience the different rhythms of the nervous system: speeding up and slowing down.

Fast Mode

Invite your child to stand up and shake their hands and legs as fast as they can, pretending to be a race car zooming around a track. Encourage them to move as quickly as possible for 30 seconds to a minute. If you'd like, join them and race along!

After a few moments, call out "Freeze!" Have them stop all movement completely and hold still like a frozen statue.

While frozen, if they are older (five to seven-plus), ask them to notice how their body feels—are they breathing quickly? Do they feel their heart beating faster? This is their "fast mode," or the sympathetic branch of the nervous system, helping their body prepare for action.

And while they are frozen (and hyperaroused!—best not to do this before bedtime!) notice and observe for yourself:

What has changed now that they are sympathetically activated?

How do their body movements change? Do they become sharper or softer? Slower or faster?

How does their breathing change? Is it fuller or shallower? Does it move to their mouth or nose?

Does their emotional state change? Do they make emotional sounds or express anything while they are revving up?

And—for the Whole Family Nervous System section later—what does it feel like to be around? What happens in *your* body while they are revved up and in "fast mode"? Do any emotions come up for you? What about thoughts? Make a mental note of these and journal about them so we can reflect later.

Now, let's melt!

Melt Mode

Okay, it is time to go into "melt mode." Ask your child to imagine they are an ice cube melting in the sun. Slowly have them relax each part of their body, sinking down to the floor in the most relaxed position they can find. As they "melt," encourage them to take deep, slow breaths, in through their nose and out through their mouth, as if they are blowing a gentle breeze.

Once they are fully melted, ask them to stay still for a moment and notice how their body feels. Is their breathing slower now? Do they feel more calm and relaxed? This is "melt mode," or the parasympathetic branch of their nervous system, which helps them rest and restore.

Play Is Regulating—Eleanor

What has changed now that they are parasympathetically activated?

How do their body movements change? Do they become sharper or softer? Slower or faster?

How does their breathing change? Is it fuller or shallower? Has it moved to their mouth or nose?

Does their emotional state change? Do they make emotional sounds or express anything while they are winding down?

Did they wind down? Or did they stay revved up? Is this typical for them? How long does it take for them to come back to their ventral vagal state?

And—for the Whole Family Nervous System section later— what does it feel like to be around them? What happens in *your* body while they are winding down and in melt mode? Do any emotions come up for you? What about thoughts?

Make a mental note of all these and journal about them.

Reflecting on the Experience

After the game, for kids who are five to seven years old, you can take a few moments to reflect with your child on what they experienced.

Ask them how their body felt in each part of the game— during the fast-moving race car (freeze mode) and the slow-melting ice cube (melt mode). Help them make the connection between these physical sensations and their feelings.

For example, you could say: "When you were moving fast, that's like when we feel excited or nervous, and our body is ready to run or jump. When we melted, that's when our body calms down, like when we're snuggling or resting."

This simple game mirrors how their nervous system works in real life: speeding up when they're excited or stressed and slowing down when they're calm or relaxed.

Remember, it is just a Band-Aid! What about their baseline?

It's useful for kids to have awareness of their nervous-system states; when you notice them getting revved up, you can remind them that they are going fast or that they are melting (or might need melting!). However, remember what you have learned about regulating Current State Baseline versus your Habitual Baseline?

We can change our Current State through up- or down-regulating our nervous system. But it is our *Habitual Baseline* that reflects our deeper state of wellness. And so, while being able to go fast or melt is good in a stressful moment, it is a Band-Aid when it comes to actually addressing our longer-held stressors and the Habitual Baseline.

Your child's nervous system also holds the story of their entire life experience. If you want to authentically integrate past experiences and improve their baseline nervous system, this is where play like Halo's story comes in.

How do we create integrative moments through play, like Emma did for Halo?

First, you might be wondering if this is relevant for your older children as well as your younger ones and at what age your kids will stop playing. It can be good to remember that even adults are playful; however, most adults have been conditioned to be serious or feel too stressed to be playful!

Dr. Gordon Neufeld defines true play (for all ages!) as being time spent in an activity where we would say: *"It's engaging. It's not work, it's not outcome based. It's expressive. It's not for real. It is safe. The will is preserved and it's within set parameters. There's a beginning and an end. And so, this is how nature takes care of us. This is where healing is manifest."*[2]

Dr. Neufeld and Gabor Maté observe that children with healthy adult attachments tend to remain playful for longer, compared to teenagers who suppress their playfulness in order to be accepted by their peers. This peer-oriented behavior is seen as a stress response and a symptom of modern culture that parents should aim to avoid. Even adults are playful! Play therapy tools are used for kids up until 12. It is not uncommon for parents to report their kids not being playful at this age, but we suggest you persevere! We have modified this work for kids up to young adults, and also, your inner child will find this healing!

You are your child's safe space.

The most important thing to first be aware of is, given a safe enough space, kids know exactly what they need to do, say, experience, and express to resolve what they are ready to!

The key to healing play and healing moments with our kids is to become their safe place—so they can re-create experiences from the past in play like Halo did! There is a saying by Lawrence Cohen that play therapists quote a lot; it is this: "Children don't say, 'I had a hard day at school; can I talk to you about it?' They say, 'Will you play with me?'"[3] At The Reconnected we say, they might ask to play, but they are just as likely to have a tantrum about the toast or hit their sibling, or if they are teenagers, they might skip school or be rude to you when you ask them a question.

There is a message beneath their behavior—if we are curious about it.

Projections

We all know this scenario: The moment your whole body tenses, you have cut a toddler's toast in half. You nervously side-glance at your kid, trying to sense where it's all heading. Yep, cue meltdown.

Moments like these can be the bane of our existence. But even when we know it's not really about the toast, it is still so hard to know what to do with the big feelings in these moments!

Projection is when kids use safe people or situations to process emotions that they have stored from a time when they couldn't express. This can be because we have been busy or emotionally unavailable to co-regulate with them when they needed it, or they might have been with someone they don't know as well, or who doesn't allow or accept their emotions.

If your kids go to daycare or school, is that meltdown the moment they see you making sense now?

Projections and Play

Children also process their experiences and create reenactments of the past through play.

Have you noticed this? They will act out scenes from the day, or they will role-play aspects of their life that they are trying to understand or work though.

If you are a parent, you will have seen the way your kids process and mirror the world in their play. Soon after a new sibling is born, your toddler might spend their days caring for dolls or "being the mum" or "being the dad," cooking, cleaning, and looking after the baby.

Children's play often mirrors real life!

Sometimes you can tell something was a big experience for your kids by the way they recount or play out a scenario that you recently experienced. The year we traveled out of backpacks, our nine-year-old often played a game with her toys where they had to choose only one or two favorite things to bring with them—very reflective of her experience at the time.

Play Is Regulating—Eleanor

And what about when your older kids start school, or meet new friends, and suddenly they might be playing out something that they have experienced? Maybe they suddenly speak dismissively to their younger sibling when they hadn't done this before, or they use certain words or tones of voice that you haven't heard before—they are reenacting something!

Have you seen this in your children's play? Sometimes it can be very obvious how the way our kids are playing relates to what is happening in life, sometimes less so! Often, we don't realize or recognize the way that our kids are communicating or showing us how things are for them.

Michelle is a Reconnected Parenting member who said she signed up for the Reconnected Parenting course just for the breathwork. She said this about her son: *"I wouldn't say there were things about my son that I thought, ooh, like he really needs some therapy or Connected Play, and then when I took time to do Connected Play with him, I was wowed about what happened next!*

"But in the first session, I right away saw him playing out things that were going on in our life!

"The first time we played together using Connected Play, he was playing out me working in the kitchen. He would hustle and play with the kitchen toys, but the whole time he was 'cooking,' he would keep his back to me, and I was just ignored. At first, I couldn't figure out what he was doing and what he was telling me, and then I realized, wow, he's playing out what he sees going on in the kitchen with me, and that is actually a stressful experience for him.

"And then it just really went on from there, and I soon realized how powerful and healing the time we spent in play was for him, and it gave him the space to play out all of these stressful moments and things that were coming up for him."

A simple moment of play together, but so powerful to hear the insight that Michelle had for her son, isn't it? He had the opportunity to say, "I feel ignored when you are in the Hustler Archetype, Mum!"

Remember: because your child's ANS is still developing, situations that are small for an adult, like being ignored by someone while they are doing a task, can be big or even life-threatening for a child! And it gave Michelle the chance to be with him in those feelings.

Kids are masters at creating and re-creating opportunities to resolve things like Michelle's little boy did. It is an opportunity to repair from moments where we might not have been there for them, but also to show them "I see you, I hear you, and I care about what happened."

Play is inherently safe.

The incredible thing about play is it is, by definition, an intrinsically safe place to explore life.

Play is real, but it's not too real, it is a safe distance from life and from the difficulties of life. It's "pretend," and all participants know it's pretend, which frees us up to fully immerse in the expression at a safe distance, which allows reenactment of challenging things to happen—lightly, and within a ventral vagal state.

We are supportive, external co-regulators when we can be *reverent* and *playful* with them. Creating the ultimate ventral vagal space means *pretending* yet never *minimizing*; we participate in a way that demonstrates we understand the importance of what is being expressed without adding heavy significance.

It means allowing ourselves to enter our child's imagination, where anything is possible. Play does not need to be realistic, logical, or follow the usual rules. Children's imagination is infinite, and to be frankly honest, it's a relief as an adult to loosen up and join them in this place on occasion!

This means that they can explore difficulty from a safe distance or a different angle. If a reenactment of a past hurt is coming up, we might view this like a releasing breathwork session, giving the child a chance to let go of an emotion, a belief, or an experience. Then a different ending or a new way of doing things might emerge.

Enactments and Integrating Core Beliefs Through Play

My Explosive Child used to play being the "baddie" all. The. Time.

He was the Explosive Kid in life, always in trouble, outside the classroom at school a few times a day from being unable to follow instructions. In his play, he always wanted to be the baddie, put in jail, and locked up. Then he would get out, only to be put back again and again. He couldn't get *anything* right. The game was deeply satisfying for him, even more so if I was the one to lock him up (in a pretend, playful way!). It was a big energy game!

Afterward, the satisfaction in his body was palpable, and we would feel so connected and grounded. He would sometimes sigh deeply in satisfaction as we completed the game.

Later he would be cuddly. Sometimes we would even get a few good days in, where he was uncharacteristically compliant and regulated.

He used the game to reenact getting in trouble, and this was symbolic of how he felt about himself. Sharing these things with me and having someone stay with him as he played was deeply regulating.

Play is more than just fun.

Just like breathwork is not just about relaxing and becoming calm, play is not just about having fun. Play is a child's language, and it can be used to express and experience all manner of emotions, and it can also be quite hard work for kids who are using play to resolve something challenging from the past.

And when kids can do this with the support of our nervous system, then magic happens. Many parents have a gut feeling or intuitively know that their kids' play is meaningful but feel that they don't have the tools or skills to know how to support their kids to process their experiences. That is what we are learning next!

CHAPTER 15

Regulating Through Play—Eleanor

True play takes care of our emotions, opens the door to our potential, and is nature's way of taking care of us.

— Dr. Gordon Neufeld

Have a think about some of the things you do when you are stuck in a stress response. Take yourself back to the Adult Stress Archetypes for a moment and reflect on how you might behave or what you might do as an unconscious way of trying to regulate yourself.

I'll suggest some common ones:

Yellers, have you ever picked a fight with your partner when you're feeling explosive? Or maybe you are trying to kick that habit, and you've tried going for a walk to burn off some steam. Hustlers, is it wine o'clock yet? Yep! Sometimes the only way to ground a Hustler down is to numb out for a bit. Avoiders, ever get stuck in a doom scroll (a doom scroll is where you flick through reels and tell yourself each time, "This is the last one," but you just can't stop)? Pleasers, have you avoided social contact because it is draining? Or gone into extreme anxious cleaner mode before people come over?

Believe it or not, all of these behaviors are an attempt to regulate an out-of-balance system. They are ways that attempt to bring us back to some kind of balance within our nervous system.

Most, if not all, of our kids' behaviors are an attempt at regulating, but often kids are punished or expected to have the capacity to control themselves, even when an adult would struggle to do the same.

Some attempts at regulating can be healthy, and others can be self-defeating or maybe downright self-destructive or unhelpful. Crying, whining, complaining, tapping feet, pushing or kicking, fighting, making random loud sounds, bored stuckness (in fact, bored kids will often disrupt things as an attempt to up-regulate!), and a lot of the behaviors that we find challenging to be around are attempts to regulate or to elicit the help they need from us to regulate.

And as kids play, they also move through stress responses and states of dysregulation—even though my son's baddie game filled up his cup, during the game, he bounced between Explosive and the Pleaser, and the game was highly charged!

Stress Archetypes in Play

Your child will move through different states of regulation—hyperarousal, hypoarousal, and also optimal states of regulation—as they play. Each of the archetypes—the Explosive Child, the Anxious Child, the Golden Child, and the Dreamy Child—all will reveal themselves in different moments. The activity that you did earlier, the Freeze and Melt, can be a reference point for you to better recognize when your child is in hyper- or hypoaroused states as they go about their day and also as they are playing out things that are meaningful for them.

And as they do, your job is to co-regulate with them!

As we mentioned, not all play is fun; when kids play, they move through being explosive, anxious, golden, and dreamy, they move through dysregulated states, and they will often reenact things that they have stored up that are underneath those Stress Archetypes. Remember the way that Stress Archetypes can be over the top of Core Beliefs, and so play can be a way to safely explore them. Play can also be cathartic, releasing, creative, expressive, reconnecting, integrating. It can be a way for kids to move toward hard feelings, to learn new things, to practice, and to understand the things that have happened in their lives.

And they will integrate the best if someone they feel safe with can co-regulate with them.

Co-Regulating Through Play

"What is happening in your body? Stay with that feeling while you are breathing, knowing it is safe to feel whatever is arising."

These are instructions I have followed myself and said to others thousands of times in breathwork sessions: How does it relate to co-regulating with our kids as they play?

As I became more familiar with play therapy as a new graduate, I began to notice similarities between breathwork sessions and play therapy. In breathwork, we stay with our experience, knowing that whatever is arising is related to our life in some way or is a pattern in life releasing. Or we might have a ventral vagal experience to anchor to, so that we can feel more resourced in life. The experience will be spontaneous and guided by our body wisdom.

Whatever arises is the perfect next step in our unfolding process.

When we stay with our experiences in a breathwork session, our bodies know exactly what experience we need to take a step toward our intentions.

When we stay with our kids in their play, they also know exactly what they need to do, say, feel, and experience, and what support they need from you to take a step toward their self-actualizing.

And when we can stay with them, we are authentically meeting them in their big feelings with genuine, congruent understanding, empathy, and okay-ness. And if you remember the key part of co-regulating—all children need is to "feel felt," as Garry Landreth would say, then their process can unfold.

When you stay with them as they play, you are telling them they are safe to feel. This isn't said verbally, but it is expressed nervous system to nervous system, in an embodied way.

What happens when we can stay with their play?

One of the biggest epiphanies I've had in my journey as a play therapist is the realization that staying with my experiences in breathwork, and becoming safe to feel anything that arises physically, mentally, emotionally, and spiritually during breathwork sessions, have made my nervous system a powerful co-regulator for other people as well as for myself—I have developed an Elder Nervous System (which we share more about in Whole Family Nervous System).

Being safe to feel dysregulation, keeping one foot in ventral vagal, recognizing reactivity, and feeling excited to move toward old stressors arising, well, it means that in the playroom, kids can rely on the adult's nervous system to regulate their past experiences.

How can you do the same?

Remember, most importantly, to be practicing the exercises in Section I! The nervous system to nervous system conversation and being authentically safe to feel isn't something we can think our way to experiencing.

Co-regulating through play means staying with kids' experiences as they play.

We intentionally stay present with their emotions, actions, ideas, and anything else they do, say, or express while they are playing, plus—and this is key—being in touch with our own physical and emotional experience so that we can feel our way into and create a shared experience.

This creates a right-brain to right-brain moment of synchrony!

Right-Brain Mirroring

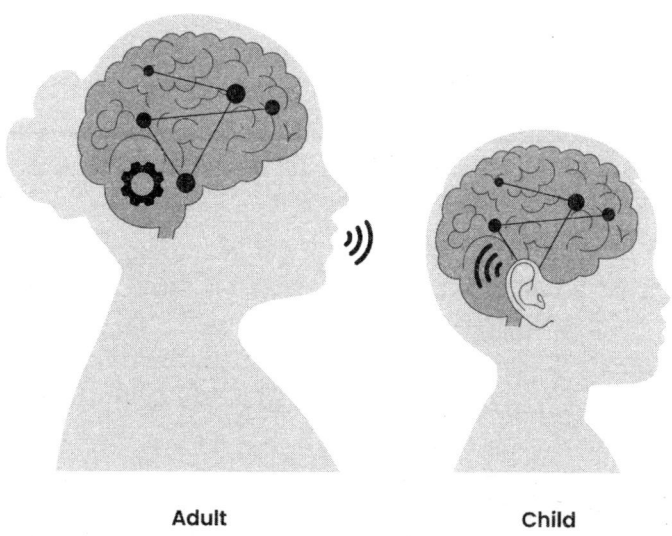

Adult **Child**

For our kids, who don't yet have their frontal cortex fully developed, we can lend them our left-brain, conscious, self-reflective awareness and presence by naming and reflecting back to them what they are experiencing. They can't give it to themselves yet, but if we can lend it to them now, they will have it for themselves later.

We can consciously become an extension of their nervous system through play by loaning them the self-aware, reflective part of our nervous system, the part that can name and be aware of what is happening. I think about verbal reflections as though I am being the child's reflective prefrontal cortex. Almost like

I am their self-reflective capacity quite literally externalized while they're developing.

Creating Moments to Connect Through Play

What does this look like?

Wait for a moment when your kids are playing and join them!

This can be especially purposeful if they are playing out something that is happening in life, or if their play is dysregulated and they are in a Stress Archetype.

Your main job is to join in and stay with their experience. This means:

- Stay connected to your own body sensations and emotions while letting yourself completely focus and join in on their play.

- Verbally reflect their experience. You can communicate that you are with them by using classic reflective play therapy tools while they play.

What does this look like? The simplest way that we can do this is by empathizing and naming our children's experience as they play. It is offering the occasional left-brain linear observation to what they are doing.

It might sound like:

You are . . . feeling sad.

You are . . . playing with the car really roughly.

You are . . . jumping as high as you can.

Or whatever it is that they are doing.

What will happen? Well, your kids will love the time connecting, but what else will happen?

It gives them the chance, like my Explosive son, and like Halo did with Emma, to do and say the things they need to integrate their experiences.

More often than not, because of the self-actualizing nature of human beings, and the wisdom of our psyche and bodies when given a safe place, kids know exactly what they need and will create releasing experiences, resolving experiences, and anchoring experiences much like we do in breathwork.

The main thing you need to do is stay out of the way!

Think back to Emma's story with Halo and notice the way she just completely joined with him in the delight he was experiencing about the game. She wasn't aware of the significance of the play, and the benefit of that was she didn't have to make any effort to not analyze his play. She didn't say anything that attempted to interpret his play. She was just completely with him in the moment.

If you think you know what your child is playing, you will need to work hard to protect them from this part of you! Remember, offering interpretations, taking guesses about what the play means, is not helpful.

No questions, no judgments, no teaching, just let them lead;[1] no agenda, just stay with them as they play, reflecting to them what they are doing while staying connected to your own body experience.

You will likely create space for play that is:

Releasing: any experience that is like an amplification or overreaction of a scenario that has happened, or the expression of a Stress Archetype, i.e., if your child is a Dreamy Child, a releasing session could be not being able to decide what to do! Or symbolic play with toys who don't know what to do next, and they are being helped or bossed around by someone who has strong ideas. My Explosive boy's "baddie" game was a releasing story.

Insightful: any experience that brings insight or awareness about why you do what you do, like symbolic play of a Core Belief (like my son and the baddie game). Insightful play can often be playfully re-creating real-life issues but then finding new ways to do things. Halo's story was an insightful story after the fact, because it integrated a previously held body memory about going backward.

Anchoring: any experience that is the embodiment of your intentions, like peace, joy, or happiness, or any experience that is new or that strengthens you in some way—like getting something you needed in the past, now in the present moment. Ventral vagal play is play that is loving, connected, inspired, settled, or content and focused. Halo's story was also an anchoring experience; he created the ventral vagal welcome that he wanted.

Creating Safety Through Boundaries

Whenever I think of parenting my toddlers, I remember this time my Golden Child was overtired, and I was trying to put him to bed. I went to shut the door, and he said, "No, not like that." He wanted the door slightly more ajar. I tried again. Nope! It still wasn't in the right place. "Not there, there!" It took a few more attempts to realize that I was not going to get it right.

And actually, he didn't want or really need me to either.

He needed a good cry! And to rage against me for a bit for not getting it right.

Sometimes when we say no, we are saying yes to the feelings bubbling underneath. Children sometimes unconsciously look for a boundary. When kids create situations that cannot be fixed, they don't want a fix, they want a "no"; they want a boundary. The sooner we can stay with them in their emotions, the better.

Reflecting on the Play

After they play and you get a private moment to think about what happened in the play (not with them, on your own), reflect on:

- What was the Stress Archetype
- What was a Release, an Insight, or an Anchor
- What happened in your body, and how it was for you while they played

You can join the conversation here: www.thereconnected.com/book.

Getting triggered by your kids' play?

Now, here is the kicker: as parents, we are conditioned to shut down the play that our kids find most healing.

In some ways this is because dysregulated states often bring out the teacher or guide in us, and it's hard for us to trust our kids' play if it gets rough or expresses upset. Maybe you have experienced this. Your child is playing roughly with some dolls and then throws one down on the ground, saying, "Bad baby!" You might feel like you need to step in and say, "Gentle with the babies."

Where are we coming from when we say things like this?

Sometimes we are doing what we think is required, based on ideas we have about being a parent and needing to teach kids right and wrong ways of behaving. Parents can easily be very focused on their role to guide kids to do the "right" thing—without realizing that the way a young child plays is often symbolic, metaphorical, or exaggerated. Play is a bit like a dream, a reflection of the subconscious. Have you ever had a dream where you are processing a feeling? It's normally exaggerated—like being completely nude in front of a room of strangers—to get in touch with embarrassment. What is big for kids can seem small to adults, and kids tend to express things with a magnification of sorts!

Of course there may be times when boundaries are important, and you should trust yourself on this; however, if you have the intention of supporting your kids to unwind their stressors through play, expect some dysregulation, and be more permissive during these times.

But more often the play is something that we don't feel okay with because we are triggered or it is a pattern or behavior that has resurfaced.

For example, I often struggled with my son being the baddie! I wanted him to also be the good guy! On some level, I was struggling with him always being the baddie in school! I wanted him to feel accepted and loved and to fit in, and my heartstrings would get pulled so hard watching him set himself up to be rejected and made wrong over and over.

I was triggered. And it meant that rather than "staying with" him, I made suggestions about what the baddie could do. Sometimes if we are really triggered by our kids' play, we might just full-out make them stop!

We shut down their attempts to regulate.

For me, there was something a bit deeper there too. The thing is, yes, he got in trouble a lot, but I also struggled with knowing how to help him! Some of this identity was developed from my sense of feeling unsure how to deal with his explosiveness beyond just trying to set increasingly firm limits. So the guilt I felt seeing him playing this out was beyond what I could stay with within myself.

These experiences of himself as a baddie were part of a dynamic that we had been playing out a long time!

Allan Schore states: "The self-organisation of the developing brain occurs in the context of a relationship with another self, another brain."[2] If it can be within the context of the same nervous system that it was created within, this is the ultimate repair. And isn't that just the ultimate gift we want to give our kids, and what we are all here for?

Before I could support him to integrate that sense of being a baddie, and in unwinding the upset, anger, and big feelings around all the experiences that had developed that sense of self, he needed me to unwind my own stored stress and create a nervous system that was more available than the self that his "baddie" self had developed within.

I had to change!

And, if you are realizing this is true for you—and you have been triggered by your kids' play or their attempts to regulate, then you are leaning in to the real magic of our work here at The Reconnected.

Whenever we reach a point in play that we can't be there for our kids' play, we can get excited that it is time for us to lean into our own breath practice, and revisit the unwinding process from Chapter 9 so you can discover for yourself:

- The Trigger
- The Overreaction
- The Stress Archetype

and then create an intention and breathe your way toward integrating what it is for you!

In this way, we can bring the perspective "They are doing the best they can with what they've got" and apply it to ourselves.

We have been doing the best we can with what we've got, and now we are ready to receive the gifts of our kids and let them point us to areas where we are ready to grow and expand within our own process.

This then gives our kids space to play out what they have been trying to, within our own more regulated, integrated sense of self. As Daniel Siegel says, "As children develop, their brains 'mirror' their parent's brain. In other words, the parent's own growth and development, or lack of those, impact the child's brain. As parents become more aware and emotionally healthy, their children reap the rewards and move toward health as well."[3]

And the spiral of Reconnection has begun!

This is what is possible in a short time if you are ready and willing to apply their practice. In an incredible synchrony, just as we were finishing this chapter, almost at the same moment, this share came in from Mary, who had just recently started using the Reconnected Parenting model:

"Since starting this course I have been having flashbacks at random times throughout my days, all the times I couldn't meet my daughter in a ventral-vagal-regulated safe state.

"These memories bring to light how in those moments the seed of a negative Core Belief could form and what my daughter might make this mean about her . . . the pang of guilt stings.

"Ouch!

"I have had grace for myself in these memories remembering, if I could, I would, and when I can, I will. On the other hand, I see the lesson/gold in these memories as clear as crystal, pointing to where my edges/triggers are and the material for me to work through.

"I love knowing now with the skills we have learned from RP, and as we keep showing up and doing this work, we begin to be able to see our edges and triggers so much earlier and get to stay in a ventral vagal state more often and for longer periods."

What is next?

Can you sense into the magic of doing your own rewiring and reparenting and then offering the same space to your child? It is profound.

This is the new paradigm, where we learn to understand what is happening beneath the surface of all our own ways of relating to the world, as well as understanding our kids better.

Regulating Through Play—Eleanor

We have two powerful paradigm shifts that will extend what you have learned so far into regulating the Whole Family Nervous System.

First, a quick note on being good enough.

Let's be really careful that none of this information or these practices become applied in a perfectionistic way.

We have found that for most families, adding in weekly or daily practices of breathwork and Connected Play, and then around that, just relaxing and doing life as you would, is the best thing.

Imagine if, instead of friends where there is mutual to-and-fro, plus natural ups and downs where you might upset each other and then make up, what if instead you had people only focused on you, empathizing with you, never getting out of sync with your needs?

Well, it'd be a bit weird, wouldn't it?

It's not really grounded in reality, but it also doesn't really recognize or support the resilience and mutuality that kids are capable of.

With small, regular practices, we can relax and allow the unwinding spaces of breath and play to simply overflow and create a spontaneous and increasingly authentic Reconnected Baseline for you and your kids. The idea is that through creating regular times of being with each other and staying with our nervous system wisdom, through Breath and Play, without changing anything else, over time, the level of regulation in the Whole Family Nervous System will overflow—and life becomes more effortless, more connected, and more fun!

What a big chapter! Let's all take a deep breath together.

Inhale.

Exhale.

Ready to learn about the Whole Family Nervous System?

SECTION III

understanding the whole family nervous system

CHAPTER 16

PARADIGM SHIFT #1, ATTUNEMENT:

The Invisible Communication Between Parent and Child

> *I have learned that my total organismic sensing of a situation is more trustworthy than my intellect.*
>
> — CARL ROGERS

In Sections I and II, you have discovered a lot about your nervous system, your kids' nervous systems, and about how your kids rely on you for regulating, physically and emotionally, and how this process creates the development of their sense of self and their relationship with life.

Now it is time to explore the broader perspective of this new paradigm way of parenting and discover the Whole Family Nervous System.

Take yourself, for a moment, to times when your kids are losing it with a capital *L*. Out of their minds. Completely dysregulated. Big feelings. Big body movements. In Chapter 12, we reflected on what it really feels like to be around our kids' dysregulation, and we all agreed that, yep, despite wanting to feel calm, most often we feel *some* degree of dysregulation as well.

Think again to what it feels like to be around that.

You might feel tense or anxious. Maybe your heart rate increases, you get sweaty, or your mind races. Recognize the hyperarousal in that description? Or maybe you feel burnt out, lethargic; the inner eye roll and compassion fatigue kicks in. Yep, signs of going into a hypoaroused state!

After reading Sections I and II, what would you say is happening for you at that moment? Most likely you will answer, "I am getting dysregulated as well." What would you say is happening if you couldn't stay with your kids' big feelings at that moment?

You would most likely say, "I am triggered," and, yes, that is a part of what is happening, but it is not the full picture.

Are you ready for a paradigm shift in your perspective?

Sidenote: If getting triggered was the full picture, can you see how easy it would be to think that as soon as we work through all our triggers, *then* we will be calm all the time, or even if you have let go of the importance of calm, that if you could resolve all your triggers, you would be able to be present to *all* your child's feelings no matter what?

Take a moment to reflect and see if you might hope or think "If I just do enough work, if I get to the root cause of all my traumas and conditioning, then I will stay with all my kids' feelings."

The desire to be a calm parent or the most self-aware parent is such a sneaky thing!

Okay, but if the activation we feel when our kids are dysregulated is not just us getting triggered, what else could be happening?

When I was a new play therapist, I definitely had the idea that my role was to be totally okay with all the feelings kids had in the play therapy room. And without bragging, I could hold a lot! I had done a lot of personal work, I could stay grounded with big feelings, and my own kids had been through a lot, so I had no judgment on kids with big energy.

I felt I could hold it all, but I had no idea I misunderstood something key.

Soon after I graduated, I had a caseload that was full of Explosive Kids, all stuck in Fight mode, most of whom had grown up with domestic violence.

And I was holding all the big feelings, feeling super grounded, until one session changed everything for me.

One of the Explosive Kids had been edging closer and closer to playing with some rough toys, in particular some rope and toy soldiers. Every week the play got a bit more aggressive, and it felt a little more heightened and dysregulated. I knew they were getting closer to reenacting and integrating the trauma they had experienced, but I wasn't prepared for how it happened! In one key session, again the play was getting aggressive, we were edging into hyperarousal, and the toy soldiers were starting to get pretty rough!

I leaned over to pick up a toy, and in a split second, the Explosive Child grabbed the toy rope and pulled it around my hands and arms so I couldn't move, saying, "I'll hurt you now too!"

Suddenly, I felt *actually* afraid; I wasn't sure if I could get out of the rope, and they had moved so quickly that I didn't feel in charge of the process anymore! In that split second I had a ripple of white-hot fear go up my spine and across my face, and a mild sweat broke out. For a moment, I froze and didn't know what to do next.

In that same moment I caught the child's eye, and I could see I wasn't the only one who was scared. That moment felt so long, but at the same time, the fear in their eyes snapped me out of the freeze, and I came back to earth, setting a boundary and moving on with the play. For the rest of the session, the room had a big elephant in it: *"What happened? I should have seen that coming! Are they okay? I don't know if that was too much! How do I repair that?"* I couldn't shake the guilt or the feeling that I had wrecked something in the therapy process.

I felt terrible about getting triggered, and I replayed it over and over in my mind the rest of the day, trying to figure out what I could have done differently. I knew the play was related to trying to process the violence they had experienced in the past, and I was gutted that I hadn't stayed safe to feel it with them at that moment.

I was lucky enough to have supervision the next day (supervision is where you meet with a mentor and unpack things you are stuck with), and I couldn't get there soon enough! My mentor listened to my recount of what had happened and, with a full of a sense of failure, I admitted, *"I felt scared, powerless, and I wasn't sure what to do! I was frozen in terror!"*

Then she said something to me that dramatically shifted my understanding.

She said, *"What do you think the way you are feeling might tell you about what they were feeling?"*

I let that question sink in.

And she continued, *"What does it tell you about how things have been for them?"*

And suddenly their play all made sense! Something sudden and unexpected had once happened, and they had been terrified, powerless, frozen.

She asked me, *"How have you been feeling since?"* I replied, *"Well, I'm still thinking about what happened, and it's like I'm trying to figure out what I did wrong."* Again, she said, *"What does this tell you about how things were for them?"*

My mind was blown. I replied, *"They were worried they had done something wrong, and that they had failed the other people around them."* I was caught up in feeling like I was a failed play therapist, but only because I had become "emotionally flooded," as play therapist Lisa Dion would say. I had thought the fear was an old emotion of mine and that I was triggered, and yes, this played a part, but getting stuck in that was stopping me from seeing what else was happening.

I was stunned and said, *"So they needed me to feel the fear?"*

My mentor said, *"That was the moment they were truly leaning on your nervous system to regulate the intensity from the past."*

A new level of nervous-system-to-nervous-system communication had been unlocked for me.

See, when kids are dysregulated, we pick up what is happening for them in our bodies; when this happens, we are physiologically and emotionally in sync with them. We actually have an autonomic window into their experience, and when I was not aware of this level of communication, I got flooded instead of seeing it clearly. In a way, the dysregulation had become the biggest energy in the room; my personal question became, "How can I be attuned and safe to feel in a way that I am aware of and work more consciously with flooding when it happens?"

It was a breakthrough as a new play therapist, but I was most excited as a parent and for the parents I was working with. See, as a play therapist, it takes some time to develop the attunement, safety, and connection we have with kids who come for counseling. As parents, we have already had many shared moments of coupled, autonomic, emotional synchronizing—since conception! The connection is there!

Have you noticed this physiological connection to your kids?

It is likely that it shows up in more everyday ways than the story I shared, which is a pretty typical trauma reenactment in therapy, but definitely not the norm in everyday life for most families. You know how sometimes you can just tell what your kids are thinking and feeling? You can see a flicker of emotion across their face and sense their inner experience. You can often tell exactly what is happening for them internally without them saying anything, and vice versa.

Well, take a moment and ask yourself, "What is giving me this sense of knowing?" You will find that your own body and emotions are the messenger; your nervous system is acting like a tuning fork, "picking up" what is happening in the other nervous system, and it activates the same emotional-somatic experience within you. For example, when your child gets really excited or scared, you might notice your own heart starts racing or your body feels tense. It happens because your bodies are sharing the same emotional and physiological state at that moment.

Remember, kids rely on connection for their survival, so it makes sense that we would be this hardwired to pick up what is happening for them. Remember how co-regulation usually involves feeling a bit of dysregulation as well? We learned about this in Chapter 11, Co-Regulation. When our kids are dysregulated, and we get dysregulated also, it is just enough so that we emotionally and physiologically match their autonomic state. Our ANS literally mirrors them so we can respond accurately with what they need. As Allan Schore's work suggests, in moments of intensity, whether they are positive moments or moments of intense dysregulation, our emotions and nervous system synchronize, creating a shared experience. Being attuned like this is part of how we keep our kids safe and emotionally secure, and how we can autonomically pick up on what is happening for them. And it's not just our kids that we are connected to: research shows the same coupling of the nervous system happens between couples.[1]

We call this interconnectedness the Whole Family Nervous System.

The Invisible Communication Between Parent and Child

Whole Family NS Connection
(Child to Parent)

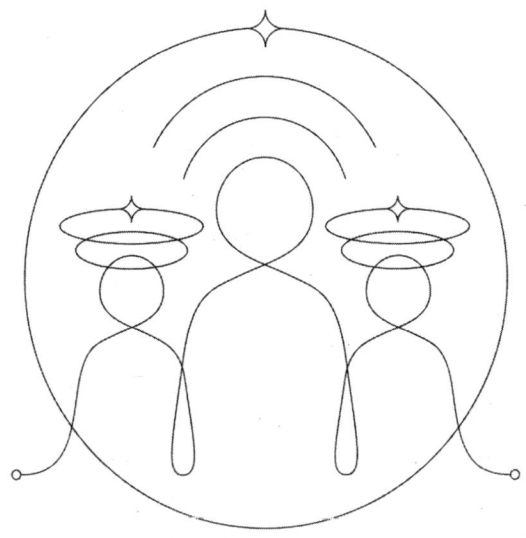

Two things get in the way of relating with awareness of this connection. Our own self-disconnect means that we are shut off from our own body and emotions. If we can't feel what is happening for us, we cannot feel what is happening for others. If we can sensitize ourselves to our body, be open to include and be curious about what is happening in our nervous system via our sensations, thoughts, and emotions, only then can we learn about what our kids are feeling in the moment or what they might be sharing about how they have felt in the past.

There is another, perhaps even more widespread and influential cultural conditioning that is at play. The idea that we are separate. Modern, Western society conditions us to be so individualistic and to experience ourselves as so separate from everything that the idea of resonance between two people, let alone literal connection, would possibly never occur to us. In fact, we are living in an extreme hyper-individualistic society, a perspective that creates separateness from each other, from nature, from life itself. When in fact, interconnectedness is our reality.

How can we take steps toward relating with awareness to our interconnection? How can we use the Whole Family Nervous System to create more regulation and awareness for our family? Sometimes we can get in our heads about "whose" stuff it is. As play therapist Lisa Dion says about emotions, "Are you feeling yours, or are you feeling the (other) person's? The answer is, both."[2]

I've found that I now think to myself, *"It could be mine, it could be theirs, but it doesn't matter whose it is; I am willing to be the one to work with it."* After all, when it comes to our kids, we are the adults, and we are the only ones with mature nervous systems—either way, it's up to us to handle it! And it is so much easier when we have the full picture.

For me, zooming out to include this bigger picture means I don't get stuck forever trying to unconsciously resolve all my triggers; it means I am aware that sometimes, it's not mine, and my nervous system is picking up some important information about the people around me. I can bring genuine curiosity and wonder, *"How does what I am feeling and thinking tell me about what is happening for this other person?"*

Two key questions help us to apply the Whole Family Nervous System in a grounded and practical way:

1. How does it feel for you to be around this person?
2. What do your feelings tell you about their experience?

Think back to Chapter 14 when we explored the Freeze and Melt game. We asked you to take a moment to ask yourself: What does it feel like to be around them *in this moment*? Let's explore what this looks like day to day and how this can play out with each of the Stress Archetypes.

Explosive Child: Hyperaroused

Let's take the Explosive Child to start with. Explosive Kids go from 0 to 100, they go into Fight mode and can be angry, easily irritable, and might lash out: kicking, hitting, and yelling. When they perceive something unknown, feel pressure or a threat, they explode!

What does it feel like to be around the Explosive Child? How does it feel in your body to be around your Explosive Kid, when you know the storm is brewing?

Most parents say they feel on edge, like they need to monitor the situation, which makes them feel a tension and hypervigilance and like at any moment something explosive will happen. When the explosion happens, it often feels chaotic, out of control, and have you noticed how everything else drops away and you have to be fully with the explosiveness? It takes over! Also, with Explosive Kids, it can be hard not to get explosive back! It can be common to feel like yelling back, and if we have to pick them up or intervene, our body movements can be harsh and jagged—it can be hard not to be rough! Do you notice that your thoughts might become very critical or absolute or extreme? With thoughts like *"Why are you always like this?"* or similar?

What would you add to this list?

Now ask yourself, What does this tell you about what your child might be experiencing?

They are likely feeling on edge before the explosion, knowing something is building and not knowing what to do about it, then out of control and lost to the sympathetic overwhelm of it all! And also feeling harsh *and* self-critical, annoyed with themselves for not keeping it together!

List as much of your experience of being around them as you can, and then ask yourself, *"What might my child be experiencing?"*

Anxious Child: Hyperaroused

Anxious children are stuck in Flight mode. I remember one of my kids had slippery eye contact when he was in trouble. I would be trying to get eye contact, and he would do everything he could to avoid it! He would run away if I didn't hold on to him and would avoid conversations about what he had done wrong at all costs. Anxious Kids can be jumpy, fidgety, and restless. As a young adult, he still taps his foot restlessly when he is stressed or wants out of a conversation.

What does it feel like to be around?

Often it can feel chaotic! Some words parents use for being with Anxious Kids are *unsettled*, *hypervigilant*, and *agitated*. You might even find yourself angry with them, because Flight and Fight sit quite close together!

Have you ever sat next to a child who is restlessly and maybe absentmindedly tapping their foot? It can feel distracting, irritating, and almost has a feeling of intolerable pressure building. You might find yourself feeling like you need them to stop, or you feel the desire to get up and leave so you can concentrate or relax! If only they would stop fidgeting and calm down, you wouldn't feel so distracted and agitated.

Write down any other sensations, thoughts, or emotions that specifically come up for you.

Okay, so let's ask ourselves the question again: *"What might this tell me about what my child is feeling at that moment?"*

Flight mode can feel like a very alert, tense, and adrenalized state that feels almost intolerable. The feeling of needing to stop the behavior or take space so you can find a calmer moment is often exactly what it feels like inside our kids' bodies!

List as much of your experience of being around them in anxious or heightened moments as you can, and then ask yourself, *"What might this tell me about my child's experience?"*

Dreamy Child: Hypoarousal

Dreamy Kids can also appear that they are not listening to us, but in a very different way from a flighty Anxious Child who is more like a whirlwind. Rather, a Dreamy Child seems to be off in their own world! They are vague and might appear to hear your requests, but then they disappear and get distracted by other things. They can get stuck whining at you, making the same request over and over or saying "please" and not being able to let things go.

How does it feel to be around?

Often parents feel helpless to do anything. They throw up their hands in despair! Nothing they say or do goes in, and they feel stuck and clueless as to how to connect or get through to their kids! The feeling is stuckness, frustration, blankness, and a strong sense of *"I don't know how to get through to them or make them do anything."* It is hard to understand why simple day-to-day tasks like getting shoes on for school can be so impossible!

What might this tell us about our Dreamy Kid's experience?

The biggest misconception about Dreamy Kids is that they are intentionally, wilfully ignoring or that they could choose to respond differently. Actually, that feeling of "I have no idea how to get through to them" is likely very similar to how stuck they feel about getting going and being in motion also. Remember, they are in a mild freeze!

Freeze is sometimes described as having one foot on the accelerator and one foot on the brake. It's being activated and stuck at the same time. You know that sense of intense frustration and helplessness when you've asked them to tie their shoelaces five times already and they haven't? Yep, it's likely they are stuck in this as well!

List as much of your experience of being around them in dreamy moments as you can, and then ask yourself, *"What might this tell me about my child's experience?"*

Golden Child: Hypoarousal

Last but not least, although they do often get left till last, is the Golden Child. They're last because they are the children who are concerned mostly about other people's experience. Not in an empathetic leadership way, but in an anxious way that doesn't want to draw any attention to themselves. They might look down a lot, and you can see they are trying to disappear. They wait till last, unable to push ahead or even mildly assert their needs or wants. They often attract an advocate: either an Explosive Child will adopt them and take them under their wing, or adults will help them.

What does it feel like to be around children like this?

Often, we feel protective and like we want to nudge them into stepping into a game or standing up for themselves. We might feel tentative and unsure about how they will handle the nudge! We might tend to check in a lot with them, make suggestions, and be encouraging. A good question to ask ourselves is, What are the emotions and sensations we are experiencing or avoiding experiencing by doing this? Usually, if you really tune in, it is "smallness." It's embarrassment or fear of being noticed or seen. It can feel like butterflies, or as though you are standing on the edge of a precipice but unsure if it's safe to step out! You want to nudge them to take the step, but you also want to hold back in case they can do it alone.

Can you imagine how this could be reflective of the internal world of a Golden Child?

They, too, are often stuck between being overwhelmed with a social situation and wanting to move forward and uncertain about how it might go. They are tentative; they'd rather come under someone else's more confident wing! It can be a full-body cringe of embarrassment to be exposed.

List as much of your experience of being around your Golden Child as you can, and then ask yourself, *"What might this tell me about my child's experience?"*

Blended Stress Responses

If your child feels like a mix of a few Stress Archetypes, that is okay. Rather than figuring out what is happening within the mind, or as a left-brain process, this is a felt-sense, right-brain to right-brain moment. The invitation is to feel what is happening in the moment with your unique child and their unique ANS.

The main question to ask yourself, in moments of dysregulation, is: *"What does it feel like for me to be around them?"*

You aren't trying to figure out what is happening for them at this point; rather, be hyper-curious, and like a scientist, describe as much as you can about what it feels like in your body; identify any emotions and thoughts that come up. Zoom out and include things that are happening for you that you might normally minimize or dismiss. Get as much detail as possible.

And then, reflect, *"What does this tell me about my child?"*

Often, if we have really zoomed out, we will have an aha that is quite insightful or that we hadn't realized might be something we are picking up.

It is really important that we use this awareness carefully; there are definite do's and don'ts with these insights that we will share soon.

First, though, let's not forget the ventral vagal state and what it is like to be in a Reconnected space with our children; after all, this is a state we all yearn to experience more of!

Reconnected Child

Ah, what a relief it is to be in the presence of a Reconnected Child. They are free, expressive, relaxed, and comfortable. Often immersed in their play or activity, they are focused, attentive, and curious about what is happening around them. Energized but content, they might sing, skip, smile, or whistle as they go about their day.

What is it like to be around them?

Have you noticed that when kids are in a Reconnected space, you also feel freed up to immerse in the things that you are doing? There is no feeling drawn into arguments, whinging, or whining, and everything is in flow around you. It is spacious, relaxed, and energizing. Your cup is being filled. You feel content. To be honest, you might even feel like a super parent or stop every now and then and think, *"This is what life is about."*

If there is a moment of connection with your kids, you are relaxed within it, and the moment feels acknowledging and connecting.

What does this tell you about kids in this Reconnected space? They feel safe and free to *simply be*. They are in a creative flow. They return to show you things when they are proud or excited about something or need some help, and these moments deepen the sense of joy or love in the moment.

And then reflect, *"What does this tell me about how a child is experiencing?"*

How can these insights help us in stuck moments with our kids?

I recall the day a Reconnected Parenting mum came on to a coaching call, upset because her three-year-old was rejecting her. She had recently had a baby, and she was juggling the three-month-old and the three-year-old, and really wanted her son to feel loved and to have a special time together.

Every time she would welcome him to play, he would reject it. Literally turn his back, become bored, walk away.

I had a sense of what was playing out, but I couldn't quite tell if she could see it, so I asked her the Whole Family Nervous System question: "How does it feel for you when he says no to the play?"

She answered, "Well, I feel rejected and a little deflated. I am not sure how to navigate the change. He used to love it."

I think you might know the question I asked next: *"What does this tell you about his experience?"*

As expected, the lightbulb moment happened! He was feeling rejected and also a bit deflated making attempts to connect and having to wait. His mum shared that he was having trouble waiting for the baby to be fed or nappy changed and was often upset when he had to wait for the baby.

When we use this perspective to help regulate our Whole Family Nervous System, another profound thing happens.

When you consistently validate and strengthen your intuitive connection to your kids, you never have to wonder, *"What is going on for them?"* again! You will just ask, *"What does it feel like to be around them?"*

You might be wondering what to *do* with what you are picking up.

Remember, the most important thing is to *feel* what is happening, and then there are some simple ways you can use this awareness to inform your responses to your child or family member.

First of all, what not to do.

Never use this information to interpret, analyze, judge, or have a hidden agenda. This doesn't create a connection. Saying things like "I am picking up that you feel *xyz*" tends to suppress and shut down rather than bring in connection, relief, and regulation.

Remember what happened when I tried to stay calm in the playroom with the aggressive play earlier? What the child needed and was asking for was for me to feel the feelings but to bring them back into safety. To regulate and integrate the intensity of the emotional flooding I was in would be to voice my experience, but from the safety of the "pretend" and the "play." "That gave me a shock, and now I don't know what to do!" I could also set a boundary around anything that could actually hurt someone so as to keep the aggressive play "pretend."

If it is not a playful moment, we can regulate the Whole Family Nervous System by simply naming what is happening for us—this is staying congruent.

The most critical things are that you are using your nervous system, feeling what is happening in your body and emotions, and asking yourself the two questions, "What am I picking up?" and "What might this tell me about their experience?" and then testing it out by naming what you feel. You can name your experience by any type of communication—verbal or non-verbal—that speaks to what you are experiencing. Use phrases that help you speak to what you are "picking up." You can say "I feel . . ." and then name any emotions you are feeling. You can also make general statements such as "It is getting . . . *xyz*" and "It all feels a bit . . . *abc*."

The Invisible Communication Between Parent and Child

When we do this, we bring unspoken, unconscious feelings into conscious awareness for everyone—in this way, we help to integrate the dysregulation that is present in the moment.

You can also take this to your breath practice—after all, it could be "yours," it could be "theirs"—regardless of whether it is in the Whole Family Nervous System and you are aware of it, this is an opportunity for you to integrate it.

Adult—Breath

Ask yourself:

- What am I picking up?
- What does this tell me about their experience?
- What is my intention for them and me? How do I hope they could feel? What would it give me?

Use the breath to stay with any sensations, emotions, or awarenesses.

Child—Play

In moments of play, you can add in this reflection:

- The Stress Archetype
- What was a Release, an Insight, or an Anchor?
- What happened in your body, and how was it for you while they played?
- What am I "picking up"? What does this tell me about their experience? How could I bring this into awareness with a playful reflection?

CHAPTER 17

PARADIGM SHIFT #2, INTERCONNECTION:

Children Will Express What the Adults Suppress

All parents know this scenario.

You arrive home from a stressful or long day out. Maybe you've been at work; maybe you were out with the kids; maybe you've had a bunch of things to juggle.

The thought of cooking dinner is unbearable. You cannot even begin to contemplate all the things that have to happen before bedtime.

You have no energy. You want to hide. You are stuck in the Avoider Archetype!

And so you flop on the couch exhausted! Hoping maybe if you just have a small rest, you might find the energy for the evening routine.

Then you hear the kids starting to play a rough-and-tumble game. You know exactly where this is heading! It starts to get noisy, and soon enough they are running into the room screaming, laughing, and playing sword fighting. It's loud, it feels chaotic, and the sound goes straight to your bones!

You feel a flash of irritation and annoyance, and you stand up, yelling to them, *"Outside! Before someone gets hurt!"*

They have successfully (sympathetically) revved you up!

Ready for paradigm shift number two? You see, it's not just us who picks up our kids' dysregulation. Our kids are attuned to us as well. At times, our kids' behavior is an attempt to regulate the people around them into a more optimal state!

Whole Family NS Connection
(Parent to Child)

The most common balancing act is the revving up of a hypoaroused parent—because we all have moments where we have gotten over it! If we are burnt out, unavailable, tired, lethargic, or flat, as in the above example, often our kids will try to bring the whole nervous system back into the ventral vagal, which requires a sympathetic boost before a down-regulation into a more optimal Current State. Maybe you are the Pleaser

Children Will Express What the Adults Suppress

parent, and your kids dominate your Fawn response and are super strong-willed. Or what about the Avoider Archetype? Maybe you freeze when your kids need a boundary. What happens next? They will probably escalate things until a boundary is set, yes?

Well, they could be trying to regulate you!

What if we are more often the hyperaroused parent? Maybe you are the Hustler (go, go, go!), or maybe you are the Yeller, and you explode or go from 0 to 100 with your temper. Hustlers, I can almost guarantee your kids have plenty of moments of whining. They're trying to put the brakes on and slow it down! They drag their heels, get confused, or are flustered and stuck.

They're freezing your Flight!

And Yellers, this might break your heart a bit, but you will have seen your kids exaggerate their flinching at your sharp tone or adopting a preemptive apologetic face. Or apologizing before you've lost it. Yep, it's the fawning that can be an attempt to dampen the fire of the yelling.

Yep, sometimes our kids are purely reacting to our own reactivity and dysregulation. This isn't conscious; remember, it's a survival need that becomes habitual, reactive ways of relating to people as we get older and have the patterns reinforced over time.

Are you ready for a deeper layer of the Whole Family Nervous System?

If all behavior is an attempt at regulating, why would our kids need to regulate us? Well, let's think about co-regulation and their survival needs. So, kids rely on us to co-regulate with them, and therefore their social nervous system is hardwired to be aware of our proximity and availability for them.

When we are disconnected from ourselves, we are not available for them—because if something did come up for them, we would not pick up what is going on for them.

In one breathwork session, I had a body memory of how, as a kid, I was *completely* attuned to my dad's internal world and Freeze response. He is a bit of a creative introvert and, like many people, was a bit shy in some situations. And in a breathwork session I had a big aha moment about how I experienced this when I was little.

When we would go out and see people, or when he was busy or absorbed in something, my guess looking back was that he was either in a subtle Freeze or Fawn response. Now, as a bit of necessary backstory, as a kid I had the label of bossy, loud, and strong-willed. And while some of that oomph is definitely my character, I had an insight recently that often my "intensity" was in direct proportion to my dad's "Freeze." If ever he wasn't available to connect with me, or if I could feel he was in Freeze, however subtle, I would get loud! And a recent aha moment of mine is that my loudness, intensity, and bigness was actually an attempt to regulate him back into connection with me.

It tended to happen when we went out of the house, because when we were at home, my dad was completely relaxed (although I am pretty sure I would have the same reaction when he disappeared into a portal of creativity that I felt uninvited to). In particular, when we were in certain social situations, his Freeze response would get triggered, and I would act out!

As a little one, I was simply attempting to bring my dad back into connection with me.

However, I also had the insight that it was actually his disconnect with himself that was dysregulating.

When he wasn't self-connected, he wouldn't pick up what was happening for me, so it didn't feel safe. Acting out, being bossy and demanding, was an unconscious and instinctual attempt at bringing my environment back into a regulated space so I could feel a sense of his self-connected availability.

A parent's self-connection is deeply regulating and orienting for a child.

Children Will Express What the Adults Suppress

Remember, they are borrowing our nervous system to regulate and to make sense of the world, and a regulated nervous system is a self-connected nervous system. To be clear, it wasn't that I needed him to pay attention to me (although that is often what happened when I acted out and possibly how it may have come across). I needed my felt sense of him to be reconnected to himself.

Think about Whole Family Nervous System paradigm shift number one.

Children elicit in their caregivers the feelings that they themselves are having trouble feeling. This means you will feel what they are feeling! The child whose inner world is suppressed chaos will feel like chaos to be around. The child who is trying not to explode will make you feel a sense of tension building! Like play therapist Donna Berry says, "What people cannot tell you, they will make you feel!"

As kids, we need our parents to be able to pick up on what is happening for us. And if they are disconnected from themselves, we experience it unconsciously as threatening or unsafe, because if they are not self-connected, they will not pick up the subtle cues that tell them we need something.

If they won't pick up subtle cues, well, generally, kids' behavior will get louder or more amped up until they are back in authentic self-connection.

Again, even authentic, congruent dysregulation can feel safer than disconnect—although upset parents aren't what we really need, it is better than nothing.

All behavior is an attempt at regulation.

Our kids are far more connected to us than we think.

So often, though, we are disconnected from ourselves, and therefore disconnected from this deep, felt attunement to our children. But our kids cannot disconnect from us, because their social nervous systems are completely intertwined with ours for survival. A similar thing happens when we try to stay calm, but authentically we are dysregulated. Sometimes the only way that we can feel calm is to be disconnected from how we are really feeling, and our kids may amp up their attempts to connect as a result.

This is why trying to be a calm parent doesn't work!

Our kids will express what we, the adults, are trying to suppress.

One of the simplest ways we see this is during everyday tasks. Have you ever tried to make a phone call, and suddenly, your kids that were totally happy previously are now suddenly very needy? This can be a sign of their social nervous system and attachment system being activated by your sudden lack of availability.

Sometimes when we teach this paradigm shift, parents start to feel defensive: *"I should be able to make a phone call,"* one parent once said to us in a huff! And we wholeheartedly agree! In fact, we are very pro parents living their lives in a way that is fully authentic and self-actualizing for them. This is the best way to show our kids what is possible in life!

However, have you ever felt like your kids are manipulating you, lost your cool with your kids, or felt really hard done by them when they are losing it over simple things like you taking a phone call?

Remember, the purpose of the paradigm shifts is to have deeper understanding of your children's behavior so you can relate to them as though "they are doing the best they can with what they've got," which instantly helps us to be able to choose our responses to our kids when they are dysregulated, rather than just losing it.

Remember, what is small for an adult's ANS (taking a phone call) can feel big for kids' ANS (suddenly feeling their connection to their co-regulation relationships is missing). Congruent, authentic boundaries ground our kids in safety and understanding of what is happening. Sometimes just giving

Children Will Express What the Adults Suppress

them information is all they need to feel safe! "I'll be on a call for 15 minutes; Dad is here for you." And when our kids feel safe and connected, we tend not to need strategies to get them to listen to us or give us the space we need to do things.

Whole Family Nervous System Reflections

What are my children expressing that I might be suppressing?

What are my children trying to regulate or balance in my nervous system?

CHAPTER 18

PARADIGM SHIFT #3, ELDERSHIP:

Regulating the Whole Family Nervous System

Whether we are speaking of a flower or an oak tree, of an earthworm or a beautiful bird, of an ape or a person, we will do well, I believe, to recognize that life is an active process, not a passive one. Whether the stimulus arises from within or without, whether the environment is favourable or unfavourable, the behaviours of an organism can be counted on to be in the direction of maintaining, enhancing, and reproducing itself. This is the very nature of the process we call life.

— Carl Rogers

The Elder Nervous System—Being the Biggest Energy

In the last two chapters, we have explored two different angles of the Whole Family Nervous System.

Through paradigm shift number one, you will now be aware that there are times when we are picking up dysregulation in our kids, and while it has little to do with our personal process, it can give us valuable insight into what our loved ones are experiencing.

Paradigm shift number two tells us that at other times, our kids will be reacting or unconsciously attempting to bring us back into self-connection and giving us the message that our Current State is dysregulated. Their behavior is an expression of something we are suppressing.

If we zoom out, what is the overall theme here?

Well, what stands out to me is in both points: if we are unconscious of what is happening for us or our kids, then dysregulation is the biggest energy in the room, and we can only be unconscious and reactive to it.

If we don't realize that we are picking up our kids' stuff, we will think we are triggered—we can't see it clearly, so we react to it. If we don't realize our kids are expressing what we are suppressing, we won't see what is happening clearly and be reactive to their attempts. Whether the dysregulation is from within us or around us, if we can't see what is happening, we are not free to choose how we respond.

When this happens, dysregulation is the biggest energy in space—we might call this "emotional flooding," but I like to think about it in terms of what is the biggest energy, and here is why.

If we can be conscious and aware of what is arising, and see it, then we are the biggest energy in the room—and we can choose how to respond to what is happening. We can decide.

At any time, you can consciously step into being the biggest energy in any given space. In fact, through the processes we teach at The Reconnected, you can become so attuned to yourself, and the strength and knowing of who you are, and how safe you are to feel, that you can notice what is happening for you, for the people around you, and decide how the entire room is going to feel!

Have you ever noticed that your energy often could determine how your kid's day goes? That if you are having a bad day, pretty soon everyone can be in the same kind of mood?

Regulating the Whole Family Nervous System

Or that if you choose to be more buoyant, sometimes you can shift everyone's mood to the positive?

Have you ever been around someone whose energy fills the room? Who determines that the space is full of a certain energy? Who "holds" it all? Whose sense of inner safety, fun, playfulness, love, or humor has set the tone?

This is Nervous System Eldership!

Child	Adult	Elder
Developing NS	Mature NS	Knows how to rewire their NS
Completely dependent	Independent	Interconnected and interdependent
Needs co-regulation	Can self-regulate	Available for the WFNS; is the biggest, most relaxed energy
Developing sense of self	Established sense of self	Sense of self is always expanding, is self-reflective, is self-actualizing

Yet we can go further than this, and this is where it gets exciting. To step into an Elder nervous system is to be available not only for ourselves and the younger parts of us, but for others.

As adults who have unintegrated child aspects (all of us do!), we can take responsibility for this now and, through breathwork, give ourselves what we never had. When we can do this, we can pass down patterns of healing that we didn't receive ourselves. *When we change like this, at the level of our NS, everyone naturally benefits.*

Whole Family NS Connection
(All Family Members)

An amazing thing happens once we start doing this work—we begin to see the people around us behaving differently. It can take some time, and it's best to be patient, and it takes only one person to create change in the Whole Family Nervous System.

As Helene shared after six weeks of breathwork:

"A week or two ago, I noticed a new calm in my body. I even craved breathwork! It's like my body knows I need it. My main intention has been to feel safe and trusting in my relationship. And, almost surprising to me, I feel much more trust and safety now.

"It's so unfamiliar, my brain is like: What's this? This can't last. But I am enjoying the new level of calm and trust.

"And I'm excited to feel more and more trusting going forward.

"In addition, I also feel like my boyfriend has changed. He has been so considerate and attuned to me lately. I really feel like he has my back; I can see his efforts, and I can feel his love for me.

"Super win! Maybe he has changed, or maybe I am just able to feel and notice it better. Not sure, but I like it!

"Being the person who is willing to go first and create change is being an Elder in your family line."

It can be incredible to observe the changes in others as we change!

Eldership is also being able to have one foot in ventral vagal, so you are safe to feel, have a bigger picture in mind, and remain available as a co-regulating resource for others. Expanding our capacity to be with our own and others' dysregulated states is some of the most important work we can do.

Parents now more than ever—and the whole world, really—need more Elder nervous systems as we navigate these times!

The Elder Is Future-Focused

Allowing ourselves to be oriented to the future rather than the past is a hopeful, energizing, and creative process.

Have you noticed that while the personal work we are doing here is integrating past stressors—which means there can be a delving into the past that occurs—it is all in the context of how we would prefer our life to be going?

This work is future focused.

Creative Elder Decisions

So, if our life is made up of decisions we made when we were helpless, dependent, and vulnerable, it says a lot about the power of a decision! Subconscious decisions are highly creative, meaning they determine a significant part of our experience—sometimes this can leave us feeling at the whim of our subconscious, or our past, or create a preoccupation with resolving the past.

We want to end this book making sure something is very clear.

All our efforts are in the service of our future vision for our lives.

All we really need to know is how we would prefer our lives to be and to know this in as much detail as lights you up! And then to use a conscious breath (rather than automatic and habitual breathing) to move yourself toward it; if there are past limiting decisions and stored stress that need to unwind, they will! But we can let our bodies figure this out while we stay most focused on how we would prefer things to be.

And we want to explore another angle for decision-making—beyond the subconscious limited ways decisions have been made in the past. If our life up until now has been based on decisions we have made in the past, our future life is based on the decisions that we make now.

So, what decisions are you making?

Given that you are no longer helpless, dependent, and vulnerable, what will you do with your life now that you are a mature, capable, conscious, and creative adult?

Ultimately, you get to decide.

You are free to choose.

Sometimes when we are parenting, we feel at the whim of everyone else in our family instead of steering the ship. Usually, though, this is the result of overwhelm, burnout, carrying our own childhood stressors, and being unaware of the nervous system dynamics at play.

When we begin to use our breath to self-connect, not only do we reparent ourselves and be the adult we needed when we were little, but we step increasingly into being creative directors of our lives rather than feeling like life is happening to us. Instead of relating to life according to the impressions we received from our family and society about who we are, we spend our time developing a sense of self that is always expanding, is self-reflective—we become self-actualizing.

We get to decide who we are.

Or maybe more accurately, we remember who we really are.

Spiritual Self

I'd love to share a story about a spiritual remembering that occurred during a breathwork session.

As the breathwork session ended, I opened my eyes, and for a moment I looked into the eyes of the facilitator. I suddenly had a sense of being more than my physical self. At the time I could only describe the experience as being aware of my soul for the first time. In that moment of self-realization, a memory flashed through my mind's eye—I was gazing into the eyes of my caregiver when I was an infant, when my awareness of who I was had to shrink to fit their perception.

It was as though I could only know myself as what they could see me as.

They could see my physical body and my emotional self. But this was only a very small, fragmented part of my entire spiritual self. My spiritual being-ness, they could not see. I remembered that in order to be with them, I shrank my own perception of myself. I disconnected from my bigger soul self and spiritual awareness.

During the breathwork session, when I was in a right-brain to right-brain moment with someone who was connected to themselves in the spiritual sense and who could see me in a way that I didn't yet know myself, well, it was like dormant parts of my being-ness suddenly popped into my awareness! They could see me, and so I could experience myself more fully.

Over the years, I have been so fascinated about what might have been happening at this moment on a neurobiological level.

Most research that informs the development of our sense of self has come from exploring impacts of trauma and neglect, and is pathology focused. As well as this, science and spirituality tend to be seen as two areas that often try not to have much to do with each other. However, I've noticed that research into development of the individual sense of self can be fascinating reading while reflecting on what might be the spiritual implications of the physical and relational findings.

One of the most common studies of the development of the self and disconnection in relationships is an experiment called the still-face procedure. In it, mothers respond to their children face-to-face as normal and then suddenly stop smiling or talking, and their face goes still for a period of time. Infants initially attempt to rouse their caregiver back into relating normally, but their caregiver, rather than responding, keeps gazing blankly at them, unresponsive. Soon after their attempts to reconnect are not responded to, the baby, realizing they are helpless to bring their parent back into connection, goes into dorsal vagal collapse, going blank themselves, and they stop trying to connect.

In these moments where there is no one to organize their experience, research has shown that babies are deprived of meaning and cannot create understanding for themselves.[1] These breaks in attunement and in *seeing, understanding,* and *responding* to the child result in the child disconnecting not only from their parent, but from *themselves*—creating a break or discontinuation from their sense of self. Our sense of self exists in connection, in being seen and attuned to enough of the time.

And so perhaps a bold question is, given that we are not (yet) an enlightened or spiritually aware society, and not many people have been truly seen in their entirety, could this perhaps be that we are collectively dissociated from the spiritual parts of ourselves? If we can only organize or have awareness of ourselves when we are seen, heard, responded to, and when someone is aware of us, could it be that we can also only relate to ourselves to the degree that we are related to? Perhaps our modern culture is experiencing a spiritual annihilation of sorts. That we are collectively and individually experiencing a disconnection from parts of ourselves that were never organized for us through the perception of the other.

This was certainly what my remembering experience felt like!

When my first child was born, I was fascinated with the question: How do I raise a child who has a connection to their spiritual self? I interviewed anyone who felt open to having the conversation. Time and time again people answered, "You have to lead by example" or "You have to have your own relationship to your spiritual self." I found this frustrating at the time, because I didn't really have a framework that was leading me back to myself—although finding breathwork a short while later dramatically changed that.

When I look back on this experience from what I have learned now, I have a sense that our degree of self-awareness, how we know each other, whether we relate physically, mentally, emotionally, or spiritually, most likely has a brain-to-brain communication that creates a strong impression on infants who are hardwired for mirrored, self-oriented relating.

And that, indeed, our own personal practice, and the capacity of our own self-awareness, is the best way for us to pass down patterns of spiritual awareness to our children. If this isn't the biggest call to action to be as self-connected and to know yourself as completely as you can so your kids have the most self-aware space to grow up in, I don't know what is.

Blessing the Child: Affirming Reconnection

When you notice your child in an expanded space—when they are expressing or experiencing a ventral vagal moment, their true self, through being generous, creative, or in the flow—without interrupting them, affirm them for a moment with a loving, fully present moment of eye contact.

While you gaze at them, feel within yourself your appreciation and contentment of their expression. This is transmitted through your eye contact, just from feeling it within yourself!

CHAPTER 19

Conclusion

Tell me, what is it you plan to do with your one wild and precious life?
— MARY OLIVER

What is the next step?

It is time for you to take what you have learned and to put it into practice!

Understanding the nervous system intellectually will only ever take you so far; it is applying the Reconnected practices of breath and play that will bring you the changes you want to see in your life.

Use Section I to create a relationship with your breath and take steps toward a Reconnected Baseline.

Use Section II to connect with your kids through play so that they have a regular touchstone to their authentic self-expression and a place where they feel seen, heard, and understood with the most important person in their life—you!

And use Section III to expand your awareness of the many tangible moments of interconnectedness and to go beyond the old ways of viewing what is influencing the highs and lows of parenting.

And jump into the conversation happening here: www.thereconnected.com/book

It is exciting to be a part of a wave of parenting that is expanding beyond the ideas of strategies and separateness and embrace instead practices that support connection at a profound level, connection to self, connection to others, and connection to the whole.

Perhaps the most important outcome is the ripple effect of a generation of kids raised in an increasingly ventral vagal embrace.

You might wonder if you can create the change you want to see in yourself and your family. Maybe you have tried many things or wonder if this information has reached you too late. The beauty of this work is that you do not need to believe you can create change for your body and breath to work for you.

While you wait for the personal proof that comes only from applying practices, we invite you to lean on our trust in the process.

Our trust in your nervous system and the wisdom of your body and breath.

Our intention for you and for your family is that you experience the truth of your interconnectedness, the wisdom of your breath, the delight of your kids as you join them in play, and that you strive for wholeness and intentional living, not perfection.

And that step by integrated step you begin to trust your breath, trust your process, and trust in life.

Now, it is time to go out into life and put it all into practice!

References

Analda, A. *Self-Awareness, Relationship with Self.* Zentium International, 1998.

Al Aboud, N. M., Tupper, C., and Jialal, I., "Genetics, Epigenetic Mechanism." *StatPearls* (2018).

Anderson, J., and June, P. L., "The Infant-Mother Connection and Implications for Their Future Health: Part 1 of 3." *American College of Pediatricians* (2023). https://acpeds.org/position-statements/the-infant-mother-connection-and-implications-for-their-future-health-part-1-of-3.

Banushi et al. "Breathwork Interventions for Adults with Clinically Diagnosed Anxiety Disorders: A Scoping Review." *Brain Sciences* 13, no. 2 (2023): 256.

Brems, C. *Therapeutic Breathwork: Clinical Science and Practice in Healthcare and Yoga.* Springer Cham: Springer Nature Switzerland, 2024.

Cerritelli et al. "A Review on the Vagus Nerve and Autonomic Nervous System During Fetal Development: Searching for Critical Windows." *Frontiers in Neuroscience* 15, no. 721605 (2021).

Chalmers et al. "Anxiety Disorders Are Associated with Reduced Heart Rate Variability: A Meta-Analysis." *Frontiers in Psychiatry* 5 (July 2014): 80.

Cooper et al. "The Circle of Security Intervention." *Disorganized Attachment and Caregiving* (2011): 318.

Cram, R. *Family 360*, podcast. Episode 32, "Gordon Neufeld: The Essential Nature of Play." February 1, 2021. Retrieved from: https://www.family360podcast.com/dr-gordon-neufeld-the-essential-nature-of-play/.

Dion, L. *Aggression in Play Therapy: A Neurobiological Approach for Integrating Intensity.* New York: W. W. Norton & Company, 2018.

Durham University. "Fetuses React to Taste and Smell in the Womb." *Psychological Science* (2022). https://doi.org/10.1177/09567976221105460.

Filippa, M., and Kuhn, P. "Early Parental Vocal Contact in Neonatal Units: Rationale and Clinical Guidelines for Implementation." *Frontiers in Neurology* 15, no. 1441576 (2024).

Fincham et al. "Effect of Breathwork on Stress and Mental Health: A Meta-Analysis of Randomised-Controlled Trials." *Scientific Reports* 13, no. 1 (2023): 432.

Glover, V., and Bergman, K. "Effects of Prenatal Stress on the Fetus and the Child." *Current Opinion in Psychiatry* 30, no. 5 (2017): 308–313. https://doi.org/10.1097/YCO.0000000000000353.

Hildreth, J. "The Development of the Moro Reflex." *Neonatology Research and Practice* (2002).

Kaiser, C. A., and O'Neill, M. J. "Early Development of the Central Nervous System in Humans." *Frontiers in Neuroscience* 15 (2021): 693964. https://doi.org/10.3389/fnins.2021.693964.

Kestly, T. A. *The Interpersonal Neurobiology of Play: Brain-Building Interventions for Emotional Well-Being.* New York: W. W. Norton & Company, 2014.

Laborde et al. "Effects of Voluntary Slow Breathing on Heart Rate and Heart Rate Variability: A Systematic Review and a Meta-Analysis." *Neuroscience & Biobehavioral Reviews* 138, no. 104711 (2022).

Landreth, G. L. *Play Therapy: The Art of the Relationship.* New York: Taylor & Francis Group, 2012.

Lang et al. "Memory Traces Formed in Utero—Newborns' Autonomic and Neuronal Responses to Prenatal Stimuli and the Maternal Voice." *Brain Sciences* 10, no. 11 (2020): 837. https://doi.org/10.3390/brainsci10110837.

Marvin et al. "The Circle of Security Project: Attachment-Based Intervention with Caregiver-Preschool Child Dyads." *Attachment & Human Development* 4 no. 1 (2002): 107–124.

McEwen, B. S., and Morrison, J. H. "The Brain on Stress: Vulnerability and Plasticity of the Prefrontal Cortex Over the Life Course." *Neurobiology of Stress* 1 (2013): 180–196. https://doi.org/10.1016/j.ynstr.2014.07.002.

Monk et al. "Maternal Stress Responses and Anxiety During Pregnancy: Effects on Fetal Heart Rate." *Developmental Psychobiology: The Journal of the International Society for Developmental Psychobiology* 36, no. 1 (2000): 67–77.

Nagai, S., & Yoshizawa, M. "The Role of Neural Crest Cells in the Formation of Autonomic Nervous System." *Journal of Developmental Biology* 8, no. 1 (2020): 7. https://doi.org/10.3390/jdb8010007.

Nichting et al. "Evidence and Clinical Relevance of Maternal-Fetal Cardiac Coupling: A Scoping Review." *PLOS ONE* 18, no. 7 (2023): e0287245.

Ogden, P., Minton, K., & Pain, C. *Trauma and the Body: A Sensorimotor Approach to Psychotherapy* (Norton Series on Interpersonal Neurobiology). New York: W. W. Norton & Company, 2006.

Porges, S. W. *The Polyvagal Theory: Neurophysiological Foundations of Emotions, Attachment, Communication, and Self-Regulation.* New York: W. W. Norton & Company, 2011.

Reynolds, P. "Fetal to Neonatal Transition—What Can Go Wrong?" *Surgery (Oxford)* 31, no. 3 (2013): 110–113.

References

Scaer, R. C. *The Body Bears the Burden: Trauma, Dissociation, and Disease.* The Haworth Medical Press, 2001.

Schore, A. N. "The Experience-Dependent Maturation of a Regulatory System in the Orbital Prefrontal Cortex and the Origin of Developmental Psychopathology." *Development and Psychopathology* 8, no. 1 (1996): 59–87.

Schore, A. N. "Attachment and the Regulation of the Right Brain." *Attachment & Human Development* 2, no. 1 (2000): 23–47.

Schore, A. N. "Right-Brain Affect Regulation: An Essential Mechanism of Development, Trauma, Dissociation, and Psychotherapy." *The Healing Power of Emotion: Affective Neuroscience, Development & Clinical Practice*, ed. D. Fosha, D. J. Siegel, and M. F. Solomon. W.W. Norton & Company, New York, 112–144.

Schore, A. N. "The Right Brain Implicit Self Lies at the Core of Psychoanalysis." *Psychoanalytic Dialogues* 21, no. 1 (2011): 75–100.

Schore, A. N. "The Interpersonal Neurobiology of Intersubjectivity." *Frontiers in Psychology* 12, no. 648616 (2021).

Sgoifo et al. "Autonomic Dysfunction and Heart Rate Variability in Depression." *Stress* 18, no. 3 (2015): 343–352.

Shir, G., and Hanna, K. "The Predictive Potential of Heart Rate Variability for Depression." *Neuroscience* (2024).

Siegel, D. J. "Toward an Interpersonal Neurobiology of the Developing Mind: Attachment Relationships, 'Mindsight,' and Neural Integration." *Infant Mental Health Journal* 22, no. 1–2 (2001): 67–94.

Siegel, D. J. "An Interpersonal Neurobiology Approach to Psychotherapy." *Psychiatric Annals* 36, no. 4 (2006): 248.

Tronick, E. Z. *The Neurobehavioral and Social-Emotional Development of Infants and Children.* New York: W.W. Norton & Company, 2007.

Van Leeuwen et al. "Influence of Paced Maternal Breathing on Fetal-Maternal Heart Rate Coordination." *Proceedings of the National Academy of Sciences* 106, no. 33 (2009): 13661–13666.

Wadhwa, P. D., and Entringer, S. "The Contribution of Maternal Stress to the Development of the Fetal Brain." *Neurobiology of Stress* 8 (2018): 126–136. https://doi.org/10.1016/j.ynstr.2018.09.002.

Wilson et al., "When Couples' Hearts Beat Together: Synchrony in Heart Rate Variability During Conflict Predicts Heightened Inflammation Throughout the Day." *Psychoneuroendocrinology* 93 (2018): 107–116.

Zoia et al. "Fetal Movements: The Effects of the Systematic Touching of the Mother's Abdomen on Fetal Response." *PLOS ONE* (2015). https://doi.org/10.1371/journal.pone.0129118.

Endnotes

Chapter 2

1. Daniel J. Siegel, "Toward an Interpersonal Neurobiology of the Developing Mind: Attachment Relationships, 'Mindsight,' and Neural Integration," *Infant Mental Health Journal* 22, no. 1–2 (2001): 67–94.

2. Theresa A. Kestly, *The Interpersonal Neurobiology of Play: Brain-Building Interventions for Emotional Well-Being* (New York: W. W. Norton & Company, 2014).

Chapter 4

1. Ogden, P., Minton, K., and Pain, C., *Trauma and the Body: A Sensorimotor Approach to Psychotherapy* (Norton Series on Interpersonal Neurobiology) (New York: W. W. Norton & Company, 2006).

2. Ibid.

Chapter 5

1. Alakh Analda, *Self-Awareness, Relationship with Self* (Zentium International, 1998).

2. Sgoifo et al., "Autonomic Dysfunction and Heart Rate Variability in Depression," *Stress* 18, no. 3 (2015): 343–352.

3. Chalmers et al., "Anxiety Disorders Are Associated with Reduced Heart Rate Variability: A Meta-Analysis," *Frontiers in Psychiatry* 5 (July 2014): 80.

4. Tan et al., "Heart Rate Variability (HRV) and Posttraumatic Stress Disorder (PTSD): A Pilot Study," Applied Psychophysiology and Biofeedback 36, no. 1 (2011): 27–35, https://pubmed.ncbi.nlm.nih.gov/20680439/.

5. Banushi et al., "Breathwork Interventions for Adults with Clinically Diagnosed Anxiety Disorders: A Scoping Review," *Brain Sciences* 13 no. 2 (2023): 256. Laborde et al., "Effects of Voluntary Slow Breathing on Heart Rate and Heart Rate Variability: A Systematic Review and a Meta-Analysis," *Neuroscience & Biobehavioral Reviews* 138, no. 104711 (2022).

6. Christiane Brems, *Therapeutic Breathwork: Clinical Science and Practice in Healthcare and Yoga* (Springer Cham: Springer Nature Switzerland, 2024), 41–97.

Chapter 9

1. Analda, *Self-Awareness*, 1998.

Chapter 10

1. Nagai, S., and Yoshizawa, M., "The Role of Neural Crest Cells in the Formation of Autonomic Nervous System," *Journal of Developmental Biology* 8, no. 1 (2020): 7. https://doi.org/10.3390/jdb8010007.

2. Al Aboud, N. M., Tupper, C., and Jialal, I., "Genetics, Epigenetic Mechanism," *StatPearls* (2018).

3. Glover, V., and Bergman, K., "Effects of Prenatal Stress on the Fetus and the Child," *Current Opinion in Psychiatry* 30, no. 5 (2017): 308–313, https://doi.org/10.1097/YCO.0000000000000353. Wadhwa, P. D., and Entringer, S., "The Contribution of Maternal Stress to the Development of the Fetal Brain," *Neurobiology of Stress* 8 (2018): 126–136. https://doi.org/10.1016/j.ynstr.2018.09.002.

4. Anderson, J., and June, P. L., "The Infant-Mother Connection and Implications for Their Future Health: Part 1 of 3," *American College of Pediatricians* (2023). https://acpeds.org/position-statements/the-infant-mother-connection-and-implications-for-their-future-health-part-1-of-3.

5. B. S. McEwen and J. H. Morrison, "The Brain on Stress: Vulnerability and Plasticity of the Prefrontal Cortex over the Life Course," Neurobiology of Stress 1 (2013): 180–96, https://doi.org/10.1016/j.ynstr.2014.07.002.

6. Peter Reynolds, "Fetal to Neonatal Transition—What Can Go Wrong?" *Surgery (Oxford)* 31, no. 3 (2013): 110–113.

Endnotes

7. Cerritelli et al., "A Review on the Vagus Nerve and Autonomic Nervous System During Fetal Development: Searching for Critical Windows," *Frontiers in Neuroscience* 15 (2021): 721605.

8. Zoia et al., "Fetal Movements: The Effects of the Systematic Touching of the Mother's Abdomen on Fetal Response," *PLOS ONE* (2015). https://doi.org/10.1371/journal.pone.0129118.

9. Durham University, "Fetuses React to Taste and Smell in the Womb," *Psychological Science* (2022). https://do.org/10.1177/09567976221105460.

10. Zoia et al., "Fetal Movements," 2015.

11. Lang et al., "Memory Traces Formed in Utero—Newborns' Autonomic and Neuronal Responses to Prenatal Stimuli and the Maternal Voice," *Brain Sciences* 10, no. 11 (2020): 837. https://doi.org/10.3390/brainsci10110837.

12. Ibid.

13. Nichting et al., "Evidence and Clinical Relevance of Maternal-Fetal Cardiac Coupling: A Scoping Review," *PLOS ONE* 18, no. 7 (2023): e0287245.

14. Allan N. Schore, "The Interpersonal Neurobiology of Intersubjectivity," *Frontiers in Psychology* 12, no. 648616 (2021).

15. Monk et al., "Maternal Stress Responses and Anxiety During Pregnancy: Effects on Fetal Heart Rate," *Developmental Psychobiology: The Journal of the International Society for Developmental Psychobiology* 36, no. 1 (2000): 67–77.

16. Van Leeuwen et al., "Influence of Paced Maternal Breathing on Fetal–Maternal Heart Rate Coordination," *Proceedings of the National Academy of Sciences* 106, no. 33 (2009): 13661–13666.

17. Schore, "The Interpersonal Neurobiology of Intersubjectivity," 2021.

18. Cerritelli et al., "A Review on the Vagus Nerve and Autonomic Nervous System During Fetal Development: Searching for Critical Windows," *Frontiers in Neuroscience* 15, no. 721605 (2021).

19. S. W. Porges, *The Polyvagal Theory: Neurophysiological Foundations of Emotions, Attachment, Communication, and Self-Regulation* (New York: W. W. Norton & Company, 2011).

20. Cerritelli et al., "A Review on the Vagus Nerve," 2021.

21. Robert C. Scaer, *The Body Bears the Burden: Trauma, Dissociation, and Disease* (The Haworth Medical Press, 2001).

22. Marvin et al., "The Circle of Security Project: Attachment-Based Intervention with Caregiver-Preschool Child Dyads," *Attachment & Human Development* 4, no. 1 (2002): 107–124.

23. Robert C. Scaer, *The Body Bears the Burden*, 2001.

24. Daniel J. Siegel, "An Interpersonal Neurobiology Approach to Psychotherapy," *Psychiatric Annals* 36, no. 4 (2006): 248.

25. Allan N. Schore, "Attachment and the Regulation of the Right Brain," *Attachment & Human Development* 2, no. 1 (2000): 23–47.

Chapter 11

1. Allan N. Schore, "Attachment and the Regulation of the Right Brain," *Attachment & Human Development* 2, no. 1 (2000): 23–47.

2. Schore, "The Interpersonal Neurobiology of Intersubjectivity," 2021.

Chapter 14

1. Garry Landreth, *Play Therapy: The Art of the Relationship* (New York: Taylor & Francis Group, 2012).

2. Rachel Cram and Roy Salmond, "Ep. 32. Gordon Neufeld: The Essential Nature of Play," family360 Podcast, audio podcast, 2021, https://www.family360podcast.com/dr-gordon-neufeld-the-essential-nature-of-play/.

3. Lawrence J. Cohen, *Playful Parenting: An Exciting New Approach to Raising Children That Will Help You Nurture Close Connections, Solve Behavior Problems, and Encourage Confidence* (United Kingdom: Random House Publishing Group, 2008), 17.

Chapter 15

1. Garry Landreth, *Play Therapy: The Art of the Relationship* (New York: Taylor & Francis Group, 2012).

2. Allan N. Schore, "The Experience-Dependent Maturation of a Regulatory System in the Orbital Prefrontal Cortex and the Origin of Developmental Psychopathology," *Development and Psychopathology* 8, no. 1 (1996): 59–87.

Endnotes

3. Bryson, T. P., and Siegel, D., *The Whole-Brain Child: 12 Proven Strategies to Nurture Your Child's Developing Mind*. (London: Hachette UK, 2012).

Chapter 16

1. Wilson et al., "When Couples' Hearts Beat Together: Synchrony in Heart Rate Variability During Conflict Predicts Heightened Inflammation Throughout the Day," *Psychoneuroendocrinology* 93 (2018): 107–116.

2. Lisa Dion, *Aggression in Play Therapy: A Neurobiological Approach for Integrating Intensity* (New York: W. W. Norton & Company, 2018), 103.

Chapter 18

1. Ed Tronick, *The Neurobehavioral and Social-Emotional Development of Infants and Children* (New York: W.W. Norton & Company, 2007).

Acknowledgments

To our partners, Daz and Ryan—the solid backbones of our lives. Nothing would be possible without everything you do behind the scenes. Your unwavering support sustains us through this journey.

To our grandparents, parents, and families—thank you for your patience, understanding, and encouragement throughout this process. Your love grounds us and gives us the inspiration to pursue this work.

To Launch Club—especially Jeff Walker, Don Crawford, and all the coaches—for your steadfast support and for believing in the Reconnected vision. Your guidance has been instrumental in bringing this book to life.

Thank you to Hay House for seeing the possibility of this book's impact and becoming our publisher.

To Sarah Mann—thank you for stepping in precisely when we needed someone to hold the influx during that initial moment of expansion and then so many more! Your ability to create precision and harmony, see the bigger picture while managing the details, communication, and being the behind-the-scenes space for us to process the ups and downs has been invaluable.

To our Unicorns team—Jesse, April, Steph, Becca, and Nissa—thank you for supporting us throughout the writing of this book and continuing to bring our vision into form.

To our Elves team—Amy and Nathan (and Nissa!)—for being the welcoming voice of Reconnected, offering a soft place for people to land when they first reach out. Your presence creates safety from the very first interaction.

To our coaches—Augie, Bel, Cassandra, Deborah, Erin, Jasmin, Jess, Jordan, Kashmira, Lisa, Meghan, Michelle, Özden, Tessa, Verushka, and Sarah—thank you for your unwavering trust in the breathwork process and for supporting thousands to take the next step in their unfolding journey.

To the Reconnected community, especially the OGs—Reconnected wouldn't exist without you. Your ongoing support energizes us daily. And to the quieter members of our community: we see you, and we are grateful for your presence.

I (Eleanor) am forever grateful to Alakh Analda for pioneering parasympathetic breath and being a true thought leader in using the breath for ruptures in early attachment, bringing nurture and the slowing down, and showing us all how to move step by step.

I (Emma) want to thank Redlyn Parker and Jude Ewer of Creative Breathwork, who, in those very first days of discovering breathwork, held such sacred space for me to find who I am and ignited the vision of the path I was meant to walk.

And finally, to the many teachers who have touched our lives—both in small and significant ways—thank you for bringing forth the wisdom we now share with others.

With gratitude and love,
Eleanor and Emma

About the Authors

Emma Johnston (also known as **@newearth.mama**) is a Master of Rebirthing Breathwork, a certified Advanced Theta Healer and Mind-Body Intuitive, and a practitioner of Yogic Science. She is devoted to walking the path of conscious living while traveling the world with her partner and their five beautiful children. Together, they are creating a life devoted to presence, freedom, and deep connection.

Eleanor Mann (@eleanorbreathe) is a qualified counselor, breathworker, and play therapist with a BA of Social Science (Counseling), a BA of Psychology (Hons), an Advanced Diploma in Breathwork, and a Graduate Diploma in child-centered play therapy. She has a lifelong passion for bridging academia, science, and spirituality—bringing a masterful and attuned approach to her teaching and practice.

Their collaboration, The Reconnected (**@the_reconnected**), is a global parenting movement for parents using breathwork and play therapy to create space within their nervous system, so they can choose their responses to their kids rather than react, and be the parent that they deeply long to be.

notes

notes

notes

notes

notes

notes

notes

notes

Hay House Titles of Related Interest

YOU CAN HEAL YOUR LIFE, the movie,
starring Louise Hay & Friends
(available as an online streaming video)
www.hayhouse.co.uk/louise-movie

THE SHIFT, the movie,
starring Dr. Wayne W. Dyer
(available as an online streaming video)
www.hayhouse.co.uk/the-shift-movie

***

THE BREATHABLE BODY: Transforming Your World and Your Life, One Breath at a Time by Robert Litman

BREATHE HOW YOU WANT TO FEEL: Your Breathing Tool Kit for Better Health, Restorative Sleep, and Deeper Connection by Matteo Pistono

CONSCIOUS PARENTING: A Guide to Raising Resilient, Wholehearted & Empowered Kids by Nick Polizzi and Pedram Shojai, OMD

FOOD BABE FAMILY: More Than 100 Recipes and Foolproof Strategies to Help Your Kids Fall in Love with Real Food by Vani Hari

All of the above are available at your local bookstore,
or may be ordered by visiting:

Hay House UK: www.hayhouse.co.uk
Hay House USA: www.hayhouse.com®
Hay House Australia: www.hayhouse.com.au
Hay House India: www.hayhouse.co.in

We hope you enjoyed this Hay House book. If you'd like to receive our online catalogue featuring additional information on Hay House books and products, please contact:

Hay House UK Ltd
1st Floor, Crawford Corner,
91–93 Baker Street, London W1U 6QQ
Tel: +44 (0)20 3927 7290; www.hayhouse.co.uk

Published in the United States of America by:
Hay House LLC
PO Box 5100, Carlsbad, CA 92018-5100
Tel: (760) 431-7695 or (800) 654-5126
www.hayhouse.com

Published in Australia by:
Hay House Australia Publishing Pty Ltd
18/36 Ralph St., Alexandria NSW 2015
Tel: +61 (02) 9669 4299
www.hayhouse.com.au

Published in India by:
Hay House Publishers (India) Pvt Ltd
Muskaan Complex, Plot No. 3,
B-2, Vasant Kunj, New Delhi 110 070
Tel: +91 11 41761620
www.hayhouse.co.in

Let Your Soul Grow

Experience life-changing transformation – one video at a time – with guidance from the world's leading experts.

www.healyourlifeplus.com

TRANSFORM YOUR DAY— ANYTIME, ANYWHERE

With the **Empower You** Unlimited Audio *App*

> ❝ ★★★★★ **Life changing.**
> My fav app on my entire phone, hands down! – Gigi ❞

Unlimited access to the entire Hay House audio library!

You'll get:

- 600+ soul-stirring **audiobooks** to expand your mind
- 1,000+ **meditations** for restful sleep, morning focus, and gentle healing
- Bite-sized audios **under 20 minutes**—perfect for busy days
- **Exclusive talks** you won't find anywhere else
- **Daily affirmations**
- Fresh content added **every week** to fuel your journey

New audios added every week!

> ❝ Driving, yard work, and housework have been **transformed**!
> – Ruffles27 ❞

Scan the QR code to start listening or visit **hayhouse.com/unlimited**

HAY HOUSE
Online Video Courses

Your journey to a better life starts with figuring out which path is best for you. Hay House Online Courses provide guidance in mental and physical health, personal finance, telling your unique story, and so much more!

LEARN HOW TO:

- choose your words and actions wisely so you can tap into life's magic
- clear the energy in yourself and your environments for improved clarity, peace, and joy
- forgive, visualize, and trust in order to create a life of authenticity and abundance
- manifest lifelong health by improving nutrition, reducing stress, improving sleep, and more
- create your own unique angelic communication toolkit to help you to receive clear messages for yourself and others
- use the creative power of the quantum realm to create health and well-being

To find the guide for your journey, visit www.HayHouseU.com.

HAY HOUSE
online learning

CONNECT WITH
HAY HOUSE
ONLINE

🌐 hayhouse.co.uk   **f** @hayhouse

📷 @hayhouseuk    @hayhouseuk.bsky.social

♪ @hayhouseuk   ▶ @HayHousePresents

Find out all about our latest books & card decks • Be the first to know about exclusive discounts • Interact with our authors in live broadcasts • Celebrate the cycle of the seasons with us • Watch free videos from your favourite authors • Connect with like-minded souls

'The gateways to wisdom and knowledge are always open.'

Louise Hay